GRASSHOPPER

NATIONAL
GEOGRAPHIC

book of
animal poetry

With favorites from Robert Frost, Jack Prelutsky, Emily Dickinson, and more

200
poems with
photographs
that *SQUEAK,*
SOAR, and
ROAR!

Edited by J. Patrick Lewis, U.S. Children's Poet Laureate

NATIONAL
GEOGRAPHIC
WASHINGTON, D.C.

the strange ones   102-123

the noisy ones   124-145

✳ the quiet ones   146-163

Final Thought   164-169

J. PATRICK LEWIS HAS WRITTEN MORE THAN 75 PICTURE AND POETRY BOOKS FOR YOUNG READERS. IN 2011, HE WAS APPOINTED U.S. CHILDREN'S POET LAUREATE, AND WAS GIVEN THE NATIONAL COUNCIL OF TEACHERS OF ENGLISH EXCELLENCE IN CHILDREN'S POETRY AWARD.

RED FOX

HAVE YOU ever thought about a day in the life of a giraffe, a porcupine, a whale, or a snail?

At this very moment, each one of them (if they are not asleep) is bustling about, fast or slow, as busy in his day, in her way, as you are in yours. Whether they live underground, on the ice, in the desert, the sea, the rain forest—or under your front porch—animals all over the world are searching for something very important: food or mates. Or maybe just the company of family and friends and the blue sky above. These creatures, like some of their human companions, seem to appreciate most of all the simple joys of exploring their worlds.

As you will see in this book, poets often try to imagine the secret lives of animals. For instance, what does any pig really need? Myra Cohn Livingston knows what makes a pig happy on a rainy day as well as in "Summertime." You may have guessed already, but Alice Schertle cleverly tells us why "The Bull" can't keep himself from always acting like such a big shot. John Agard lists angry names for an alligator, but warns us not to use any of them until we have crossed the river safely!

The poems in these pages resonate with wonder at the variety, beauty, and strangeness of the animal world around us. As you read them, you may think, *I never thought of a caterpillar, a starfish, or an elephant in that way before.* That's what all poets hope you will say after you have read their poems. And if the poet succeeds, then you may remember a line or two—and the animal for whom the lines were written—long after you have finished reading the poem.

This book is not for reading straight through. Pick it up anytime. Choose a poem and then read it out loud: You want your ears to have as much fun as your mouth is having. Take the book to the doctor, the dentist, or put it in your book bag. Once you have opened it, you are likely to find words that are not so much a description as a revelation.

And the pictures are pretty nice, too!

—*J. Patrick Lewis, U.S. Children's Poet Laureate*

WELC
TO THE
WORLD

AMERICAN ROBIN

OME

The Egg

If you listen very carefully, you'll hear the chicken hatching.
At first there scarcely was a sound, but now a steady scratching;
and now the egg begins to crack, the scratching begins to quicken,
as anxiously we all await the exit of the chicken.

And now a head emerges from the darkness of the egg,
and now a bit of fluff appears, and now a tiny leg,
and now the chicken's out at last, he's shaking himself loose.
But, wait a minute, that's no chicken . . . goodness, it's a goose.

—Jack Prelutsky

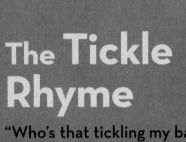

The **Tickle Rhyme**

"Who's that tickling my back?" said the wall.
"Me," said a small
Caterpillar.
"I'm learning
To crawl."

—Ian Serraillier

What's a Caterpillar?

Little
but a fly
in waiting.

—Graham Denton

MONARCH
CATERPILLAR

Cocoon

The little caterpillar creeps
Awhile before in silk it sleeps.
It sleeps awhile before it flies,
And flies a while before it dies,
And that's the end of three good tries.

—David McCord

MONARCH BUTTERFLY CHRYSALIS

BALI SARDINES

Haiku

Dancing through the waves,
ballerinas of the blue—
the ocean their stage.

—*Joan Bransfield Graham*

THE BIG

ONES

Buffalo Dusk

The buffaloes are gone.
And those who saw the buffaloes are gone.
Those who saw the buffaloes by the thousands and how they
    pawed the prairie sod into dust with their hoofs,
    their great heads down pawing on in a great pageant
    of dusk,
Those who saw the buffaloes are gone.
And the buffaloes are gone.

—*Carl Sandburg*

Wedding Bears

A panda by the name of Ling-
Ling met another panda, Ping.
They fell in love the first of spring
And hand in hand, Ling-Ling and Ping
Planned a panda wedding-ding.
A fling,
A ring,
A wedding-ding!
The sun was shining.
So was Ling-
Ling standing
Hand in hand with Ping.

    —J. Patrick Lewis

GIANT PANDAS

The Purple Cow

I never saw a Purple Cow,
  I never hope to see one,
But I can tell you anyhow,
  I'd rather see than be one.

—Gelett Burgess

Cow

The cow
Coming
Across the grass
Moves
Like a mountain
Toward us;
Her hipbones
Jut
Like sharp
Peaks
Of stone,
Her hoofs
Thump
Like dropped
Rocks:
Almost
Too late
She stops.

—Valerie Worth

A Farmer's Boy

They strolled down the lane together,
The sky was studded with stars—
They reached the gate in silence
And he lifted down the bars—
She neither smiled nor thanked him
Because she knew not how;
For he was just a farmer's boy
And she was a jersey cow.

—Anonymous

VALDOSTANA COWS

The Cow

The friendly cow all red and white,
　　I love with all my heart;
She gives me cream with all her might,
　　To eat with apple tart.

She wanders lowing here and there,
　　And yet she cannot stray,
All in the pleasant open air,
　　The pleasant light of day;

And blown by all the winds that pass
　　And wet with all the showers,
She walks among the meadow grass
　　And eats the meadow flowers.

—Robert Louis Stevenson

The Pasture

I'm going out to clean the pasture spring;
I'll only stop to rake the leaves away
(And wait to watch the water clear, I may):
I sha'n't be gone long.—You come too.

I'm going out to fetch the little calf
That's standing by the mother. It's so young
It totters when she licks it with her tongue.
I sha'n't be gone long.—You come too.

—Robert Frost

Dear Orangutan,

Three cheers to you, man of the forest.
You arrived here long before us.
You paved the way; you saw it through.
Now nice to have someone like you
sitting in our family tree.

Sincerely, from your cousin,
Me

—David Elliott

mOOse

To introduce
the world of moose,
gather woodlands
stream and spruce.
Add antlers
scooping bits of sky;
pause to watch
in wonder—*sigh*,
as he dines on aspen, fir
carefully watching
out for her.

—*Rebecca Kai Dotlich*

Song of a Bear

There is danger where I move my feet.
I am a whirlwind. There is danger where I move my feet.
I am a gray bear.
When I walk, where I step lightning flies from me.
Where I walk, one to be feared.
Where I walk, long life.
One to be feared I am.
There is danger where I walk.

—A Navajo poem

Grandpa Bear's Lullaby

The night is long
But fur is deep.
You will be warm
In winter sleep.

The food is gone
But dreams are sweet
And they will be
Your winter meat.

The cave is dark
But dreams are bright
And they will serve
As winter light.

Sleep, my little cubs, sleep.

—Jane Yolen

GRIZZLY BEARS

Elephant

The elephant carries a great big trunk;
He never packs it with clothes;
It has no lock and it has no key,
But he takes it wherever he goes.

—*Anonymous*

Elephant

A threatening cloud, plumped fat and gray,
Snorts a thunder, rains a spray
And billows puffs of dust away—
A weather maker every day.

—*Ann Whitford Paul*

Eletelephony

Once there was an elephant,
Who tried to use the telephant—
No! No! I mean an elephone
Who tried to use the telephone—
(Dear me! I am not certain quite
That even now I've got it right.)
Howe'er it was, he got his trunk
Entangled in the telephunk;
The more he tried to get it free,
The louder buzzed the telephee—
(I fear I'd better drop the song
Of elephop and telephong!)

—*Laura E. Richards*

Anthology

So many stories
Locked inside the amber eye
Of one elephant

—*Tracie Vaughn Zimmer*

ASIAN ELEPHANT

The Whales
Off Wales

With walloping tails, the whales off Wales
Whack waves to wicked whitecaps.
And while they snore on their watery floor,
They wear wet woolen nightcaps.

The whales! the whales! the whales off Wales,
They're always spouting fountains.
And as they glide through the tilting tide,
They move like melting mountains.

—X. J. Kennedy

HUMPBACK WHALE

Polar Bear Rap

Weather be chillin',
Weather be nice
Whether we swimmin'
Up under de ice.

Weather be sleetin',
Weather be snow
Whether we stayin'
But we gotta go.

Weather be nuttin'
'Less me 'n' you
Bust on outta this
Nuttin' much zoo.

—*J. Patrick Lewis*

Polar Bear

Every time
I stand and stare
At the big
White polar bear,
I wonder
While he's
Swimming there,
If he has on
Long underwear.

—*Leland Blair Jacobs*

Moody Guy

Boulders for shoulders,
Elegant horn—
A pointed reminder of the
Unicorn,
Thick leg-pillars bruising tawny
Yellow grass

In huge hide shoes,
Nobody argues

This is a colossal
Holdover from
Earth's primeval swamp.

But
Even so, I know
A rhino when I
See one, and this is the time not
To.

—Avis Harley

The White Rhinoceros

I took a number 7 bus
To see the White Rhinoceros.

I rang the bell. He let me in
And said, "Hello. How have you been?"

I told him all my hopes and fears.
He looked at me and flicked his ears.

I told him all my fears and hopes.
He handed me two telescopes.

I questioned him about his horn.
He said, "Before the world was born."

"But how," I asked him, "can that be?"
He said, "And now it's time for tea."

I left his house at half-past-four.
He chuckled as he shut the door.

—Stephen Mitchell

Tiger

There was a young lady of Niger
Who smiled as she rode on a tiger.
    They returned from the ride
    With the lady inside—
And the smile on the face of the tiger.

—Anonymous

Giraffe

How lucky
To live
So high
Above
The body,
Breathing
At heaven's
Level,
Looking
Sun
In the eye;
While down
Below
The neck's
Precarious
Stair,
Back, belly,
And legs
Take care
Of themselves,
Hardly
Aware
Of the head's
Airy
Affairs.

—Valerie Worth

Above All

Celebrate these
Long-standing giraffes,
Opening
Up clouds and eaves-
Dropping on the wind!

Far
Removed
In airy
Elegance,
Nibbling on high, they
Decorate the
Sky.

—Avis Harley

The Hippopotamus

I shoot the Hippopotamus
With bullets made of platinum.
Because if I used leaden ones
His hide is sure to flatten 'em.

—Hilaire Belloc

HIPPOPOTAMUS

The Horses

It has turned to snow in the night.
The horses have put on
their long fur stockings
and they are wearing
fur caps with high necks
out of which the device
of their ears makes four statues.
Their tails have caught flecks
of snow and hang down
loose as bedsheets.
They stand nose to nose
in the blue light that coats
the field before sunup
and rub dry their old kisses.

—Maxine Kumin

The Horseman

I heard a horseman
　　Ride over the hill;
The moon shone clear,
　　The night was still;
His helm was silver,
　　And pale was he;
And the horse he rode
　　Was of ivory.

—Walter de la Mare

Horses

Back and forth
and up and down
horses' tails go switching.

Up and down
and back and forth
horses' skins go twitching.

Horses do
a lot of work
to keep themselves from itching.

—*Aileen Fisher*

The **White Horse**

The youth walks up to the white horse, to put its halter on
and the horse looks at him in silence.
They are so silent, they are in another world.

—*D. H. Lawrence*

WESTERN LOWLAND GORILLA

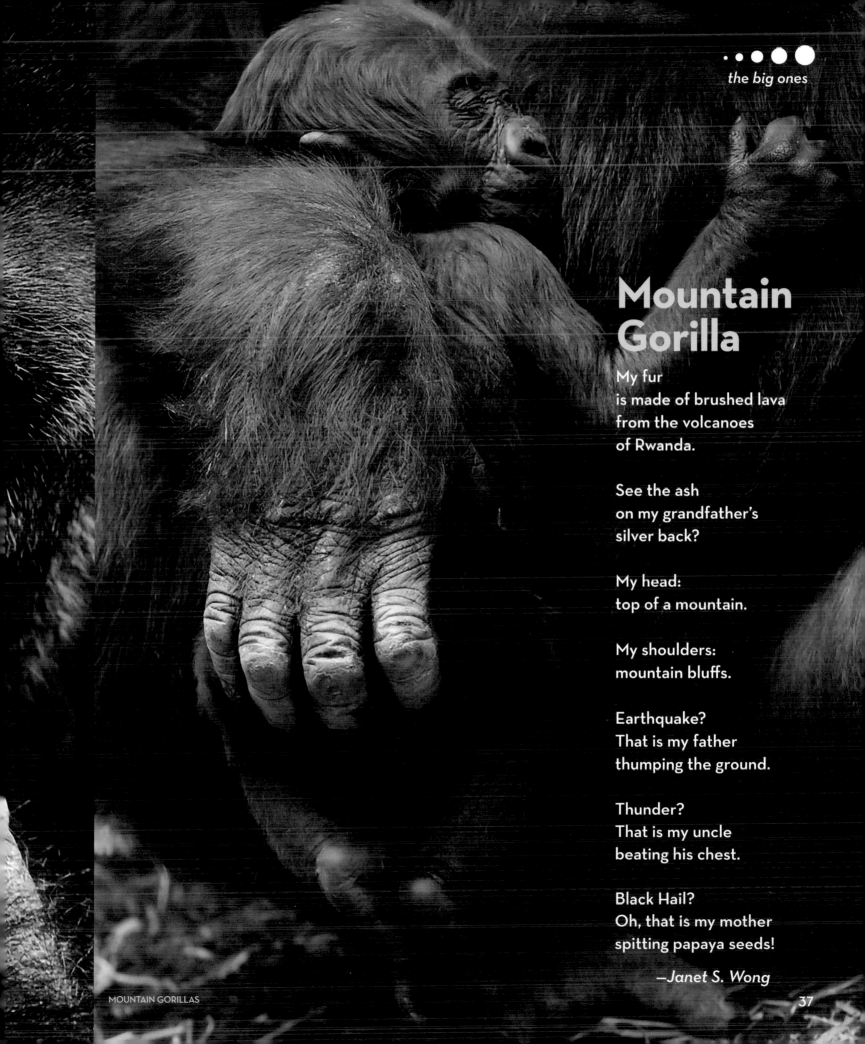

Mountain Gorilla

My fur
is made of brushed lava
from the volcanoes
of Rwanda.

See the ash
on my grandfather's
silver back?

My head:
top of a mountain.

My shoulders:
mountain bluffs.

Earthquake?
That is my father
thumping the ground.

Thunder?
That is my uncle
beating his chest.

Black Hail?
Oh, that is my mother
spitting papaya seeds!

—Janet S. Wong

THE LITTLE ONES

Ladybug

Smaller
than a button,
bigger than a spot
this crimson queen
with midnight polished
polka dots
journeys in
her ruby shell,
across
the walks,
along
the cracks,
among
the petals of a rose—
carefully,
tenderly she goes.

—*Rebecca Kai Dotlich*

Ants

One and one and one and one
    Dead leaves
    Dead crickets
One ant alone can't pick it
    up
can't drag this meal to our busy nest
But one and one and one and one
    Together we tow
    Together we know
any time of day this is so:
One and one and one and one
    is the best way
    to get things done

        —Marilyn Singer

Solitude

There now, where the first crumb
Falls from the table
You think no one hears it
As it hits the floor

But somewhere already
The ants are putting on
Their Quakers' hats
And setting out to visit you.

        —Charles Simic

WEAVER ANT

41

Dragonfly

It skims the pond's surface,
searching for gnats, mosquitoes, and flies.
Outspread wings blur with speed.
It touches down
and stops to sun itself on the dock.
Wings flicker and still:
stained-glass windows
with sun shining through.

—*Georgia Heard*

DAMSELFLY

Grasshoppers Three

Grasshoppers three a-fiddling went,
Hey-ho, never be still!
They paid no money toward their rent
But all day long with elbow bent
They fiddled a tune called "Rill-a-be, rill-a-be"
Fiddled a tune called "Rill-a-be-rill."

—An old song

GRASSHOPPERS

43

Little Fish

The tiny fish enjoy themselves
in the sea.
Quick little splinters of life,
their little lives are fun to them
in the sea.

—*D. H. Lawrence*

BLUESTREAK
FUSILIER

GORGONIAN CORAL AND
FEATHER STAR

CATERPILLAR

The Caterpillar

The caterpillar's not a cat.
It's very small
And short and fat,
And with those beady little eyes
Will never win a beauty prize.
The caterpillar's brain is small—
It only knows to eat and crawl.
But for this creepy bug don't cry,
It soon will be a butterfly.

—Douglas Florian

Caterpillar

Caterpillar. Bulgy. Brown.
Creeping up the rose.
Soon he will be beautiful
In his party clothes.

—Tony Johnston

The **Butterfly**

A book of summer is the butterfly:
The print is small and hard to read,
The pages ruffle in the wind,
And when you close them up they die.

—John Fuller

Butterfly

What is a butterfly?
At best
He's but a caterpillar
Dressed.

—Benjamin Franklin

TIGER SWALLOWTAIL
BUTTERFLY

Cockroach
sandwich

Cockroach sandwich
For my lunch
Hate the taste
But love the crunch!

—Colin McNaughton

The Scorpion

The scorpion is as black as soot.
He dearly loves to bite;
He is a most unpleasant brute
To find in bed, at night.

—Hilaire Belloc

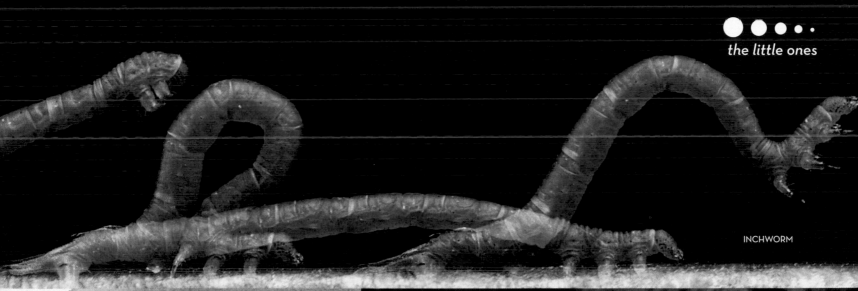

INCHWORM

Inch**worm**

You have no reason for alarm
should an inchworm climb your arm.
Hunching, stretching, does no harm.

You're just an observation post
he'll cling on for a minute at most,
then make the switch to another host.

—*Michael J. Rosen*

Inch by Inch

Wiggle
over here, dear—
scribble through mud puddles
with me by fractions and inches
of spring.

—*Rebecca Kai Dotlich*

Rich Lizard

The rich lizard
shed his skin
of silver coins,
dropping them
in the dry grass.
Strange-wild thoughts
shook him,
warming his blood
to grander things,
and he tore himself
loose—
ran off,
leaving behind
his wealth of cold coins.

—*Deborah Chandra*

GREEN ANOLE

49

The Chipmunk

My friends all know why I am shy,
But the chipmunk is twice as shy as I.
He moves with flickering indecision
Like stripes across the television.
He likes the shadow of a cloud,
Or Emily Dickinson read aloud.

—Ogden Nash

EASTERN CHIPMUNK

Squirrel Forgets

Where
where
where
did I bury
that nut,

that sweet plump
nut that I carried
away?

Where
did I stop?
Where did I drop

that fat ripe nut
that I saved for
today?

Did I hide it
deep and far, or
near?

And why's a new green
nut tree growing
here?

—Lilian Moore

Spruce Woods

It's so still
today that a
dipping bough means
a squirrel
has gone through.

—A. R. Ammons

Polliwogs

Come see
What I found!
Chubby commas,
Mouths round,
Plump babies,
Stubby as toes.
Polliwogs!
Tadpoles!

Come see
What I found!
Frogs-in-waiting—
Huddled in puddles,
Snuggled in mud.

—*Kristine O'Connell George*

GLASS FROGS

Oh the Toe-Test!

The fly, the fly,
in the wink of an eye,
can taste with his feet
if the syrup is sweet
or the bacon is salty.
Oh is it his fault he
gets toast on his toes
as he tastes as he goes?

—*Norma Farber*

The
Spider
Is a Lovely
Lady

The spider is a lovely lady.
She knows just what to do.
She weaves a dainty web
to catch the morning dew.

The spider is a lovely lady.
She lives among the trees.
Her babies are so small
they float upon the breeze.

They spin a silken thread
that lifts them in the air.
"Take me home," they whisper.
And it brings them there.

—*Frank Asch*

CUCUMBER SPIDER

I Am a Snail

I am a Snail
And my tell-trail
Is what I leave
Behind. Believe
Me when I say
I'm built this way—
My tummy slime
Is scummy. I'm
A crawling mess
Of stickiness,
And in my wake,
Make no mistake,
Is my distur-
bing signature.

—Anonymous

Riddle

No matter where I travel.
No matter where I roam.
No matter where I find myself.
I always am at home.

Sniffed the snail
In its shell,
"This fact is true
Of me as well."

—Mary Ann
Hoberman

from The Snail

To grass, or leaf, or fruit, or wall,
The Snail sticks close, nor fears to fall,
As if he grew there, house and all
Together.

—William Cowper

Snail

The snail is skilled at going slow:
   It spans the earth by inches.
Where it has gone a trail will show.
   Its brave horn seldom flinches.

A dome of chalk upon its back,
   It lets a mayfly ride it
And when at night it goes to sleep
   It curls itself inside it.

—X. J. Kennedy

Bee

You want to make some honey?
All right. Here's the recipe.
Pour the juice of a thousand flowers
Through the sweet tooth of a Bee.

—*X. J. Kennedy*

Move Over

Big
burly
bumblebee
buzzing
through the grass,
move over.

Black and
yellow
clover rover,
let me pass.

Fat and
furry
rumblebee
loud on the
wing,
let me
hurry
past
your sting.

—*Lilian Moore*

The Pedigree of Honey

The Pedigree of Honey
Does not concern the Bee—
A Clover, any time, to him,
Is Aristocracy—

—**Emily Dickinson**

A Bee

A bee
staggers out
of the peony.

—*Matsuo Basho, translated
by Robert Hass*

A Mouse of My Acquaintance

He thinks whatever's mine is his.
He lives with me but pays no rent,
And now I learn the mouse's Ms.,
To my utter astonishment,
Sleeps in my shoe.

The sneaky lodger and his wife,
Who may be sweet for all I know,
Have made a shambles of my life:
Two pickpockets on tippy-toe.
What can I do?

A mouse alone might be a friend;
Two mice are more than just one pair.
Two mice? That pair will never end.
The last time that I counted there
Were twenty-two!

—Anonymous

The City Mouse and the Garden Mouse

The city mouse lives in a house;
    The garden mouse lives in a bower,
He's friendly with the frogs and toads,
    And sees the pretty plants in flower.

The city mouse eats bread and cheese;
    The garden mouse eats what he can;
We will not grudge him seeds and stalks,
    Poor little, timid, furry man.

—Christina Georgina Rossetti

HOUSE MOUSE

Hamster Hide-and-Seek

Over my arm
she softly flows—
cinnamon coat
and whiskery nose.

With marble eyes
she stops and peeks;
lets me stroke
her knapsack cheeks.

Then ripple-of-fur
takes her leave
to probe new roads
inside my sleeve.

—*Avis Harley*

RUSSIAN DWARF HAMSTER

THE WING

E

D

ONES

Three Little Owls Who Sang Hymns

There were three little owls in a wood
Who sang hymns whenever they could;
What the words were about
One could never make out,
But one felt it was doing them good.

—Anonymous

A **Wise** Old Owl

A wise old owl lived in an oak
The more he saw the less he spoke
The less he spoke the more he heard.
Why can't we all be like that wise old bird?

—*A nursery rhyme*

Haiku

*Listen . . . in the woods
a snowy owl is eating
the wind's syllable*

—*Anonymous*

I Talk With the Moon

I talk with the moon, said the owl
While she lingers over my tree
I talk with the moon, said the owl
And the night belongs to me.

I talk with the sun, said the wren
As soon as he starts to shine
I talk with the sun, said the wren
And the day is mine.

—*Beverly McLoughland*

Gray Goose

Gray mama goose
in a tizzy,
honk-honk-honking herself dizzy,
can't find her gosling,
she's honking and running,
webbed feet slapping,
all wild waddle,
her feathers a muddle,
splashing through puddles,
wings flapping. . . .

Ah,
there's her gold baby,
all fuzz,
napping.

—Julie Larrios

CANADA GEESE

Moon Geese

You pressed the cold
circle against my eye,
I jumped back,
the moon so close
I thought it stuck
to the end of the telescope.

Then a dark fleck showed,
grew darker, longer,
and I shouted at
six geese rowing
across a full moon.

—Ann Turner

CANADA GEESE

What Was That?

Ducks catapult into the water.
Herons' stilt legs trail
their sudden flight to
somewhere safer.

Flat shells smack the lake,
bony heads resurface,
stare at forsaken thrones.

What was that?

Maybe nothing.
A dog barked,
a child ran,
a turtle slipped.
All's clear
on the lip of the lake,
for now.

—*David L. Harrison*

De Grey Goose

The preacher went a-huntin'
Lawd, Lawd, Lawd.
The preacher went a-huntin'
Lawd, Lawd, Lawd.
(Repeat pattern for each verse)

He carried 'long his shotgun.
'Long came a grey goose.
The gun went "a-boo-loo!"
Down came a grey goose.
He was six weeks a-fallin'.
Then they give a feather-pickin'.
Yo' wife an' my wife.
They was six weeks a-pickin'.
So they put him on to parboil.
He was six weeks a-boilin'.
So they put him on the table.
Fork couldn't stick him.
Knife couldn't cut him.
So they took him to the hog-pen,
Broke the sow's teeth out.

—*Huddie Ledbetter*

Puzzling

Here's a fact that will cause you to frown—
Instead of growing up a goose grows down.

—*William Cole*

CANADA GOOSE

Blue Jay

Blue Jay raises his
crest and shrieks out to the flock,
"Hawk incoming! Fight!"

—Janet S. Wong

Dust of Snow

The way a crow
Shook down on me
The dust of snow
From a hemlock tree
Has given my heart
A change of mood
And saved some part
Of a day I had rued.

—Robert Frost

CROW

The Blackbird

In the far corner
close by the swings,
every morning
a blackbird sings.

His bill's so yellow,
His coat's so black,
that he makes a fellow
whistle back.

Ann, my daughter,
thinks that he
sings for us two
especially.

—Humbert Wolfe

EURASIAN BLACKBIRD

The Eagle

He clasps the crag with crooked hands
Close to the sun in lonely lands,
Ringed with the azure world, he stands.

The wrinkled sea beneath him crawls;
He watches from his mountain walls,
And like a thunderbolt he falls.

—*Alfred, Lord Tennyson*

BALD EAGLE

Mother's Plea

Silence sirens.

Hush all horns.

Quiet rumbling

traffic roars.

Please
city

have
some
pity.

Promise me

not
one
more
beep?

My newborn

pigeons
need
their
sleep.

—Lee Bennett Hopkins

Coastal Bats

**Coastal bats
enjoy the view
from high on cliffs
in misty caves.
They like to watch
the frisky waves
when the sea is wild
and misbehaves.**

—*Calef Brown*

VAMPIRE BAT

A Warbler

In the sedge a tiny song
Wells and trills the whole day long;
In my heart another bird
Has its music heard.

As I watch and listen here,
Each to each pipes low and clear;
But when one has ceased to sing,
Mine will still be echoing.

—Walter de la Mare

The Saddest Noise

The saddest noise, the sweetest noise,
    The maddest noise that grows,—
The birds, they make it in the spring,
    At night's delicious close.

—Emily Dickinson

Birds in the Garden

Greedy little sparrow,
    Great big crow,
Saucy little chickadee,
    All in a row.

Are you very hungry,
    No place to go?
Come and eat my breadcrumbs,
    In the snow.

—Anonymous

from Sing-Song

"*Kookoorookoo! kookoorookoo!*"
Crows the cock before the morn;
"*Kikirikee! kikirikee!*"
Roses in the east are born.

"*Kookoorookoo! kookoorookoo!*"
Early birds begin their singing;
"*Kikirikee! kikirikee!*"
The day, the day, the day is springing.

—Christina Georgina Rossetti

Inuit Song

SEA GULL
who flaps his wings
over my head
        in the blue air,

you GULL up there
dive down
        come here
take me with you
        in the air!

Wings flash by
my mind's eye
and I'm up there sailing
in the cool air,
        a-a-a-a-a-ah,

            in the air.

—translated by Edward Field,
after Nakasuk

Haiku

Frantic sandpiper
high tides erasing
her footnotes

—Anonymous

BLACK-HEADED GULL

Visitor

A spark, a glint,
  a glimpse
   of pixie tidbit.
Bright flits, brisk zips,
  a green-gray blur,
  wings, zings, and *whirr*—

I just heard
  a humming of bird.

       —*Kristine O'Connell George*

You Can Talk About Your Hummingbirds

on hot june afternoons   sticking
                                  noses

into sweet clematis blooms
and
talk about goldfinch feathers
       against green leaves
but
during winter
    winter mornings
we are
    the gray birds of the yards

     sometimes in march
the only moving
     things on frozen
          air

    —*Arnold Adoff*

Hummingbird

I'm The Nectar Inspector,
Sweetness Detector–
I sip–
I don't sniff.
I love juice
not perfume.
In its deep-throated scarlet
cup of a bud
(Beardtongue) Penstemon's
my favorite brew!

    —*Janet S. Wong*

Haiku

A bitter morning:
sparrows sitting together
without any necks.

—*J. W. Hackett*

WHITE-THROATED SPARROW

Arrivals

The swallows light
on sloping wires,
then tails flicking
they slice the clouds
more delicate than surgeons,
let summer in.

—*Ann Turner*

BARN SWALLOW

The **White Egret**

The white egret

marks time

on

one

leg

then

the

other.

—Paul Janeczko

GREAT EGRET

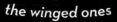

The Parrot

I am the pirate's parrot,
I sail the seven seas
And sleep inside the crow's nest
Don't look for me in trees!

I am the pirate's parrot,
A bird both brave and bold.
I guard the captain's treasure
And count his hoard of gold.

—*Anonymous*

BLUE AND YELLOW MACAW

THE WATER ONES

Penguins

Penguins waddle.
Penguins stroll
All around
The cold South Pole.

Penguins slide.
Penguins swim.
Penguins never
Look too slim.

Penguins play.
Penguins dress
Always in
Their Sunday best.

—*Charles Ghigna*

The Penguin

The penguin sits upon the shore
And loves the little fish to bore.
He has one enervating joke
That would a very saint provoke:
"The *pen*-guin's mightier than the *sword*-fish."
He tells this daily to the bored fish
Until they are so weak they float
Without resistance down his throat.

—*Oliver Herford*

Lost in the
Cold

When a Penguin got lost at Peng. Station,
She was told at South Pole Information,
   "Next stop: Icy Pool,
   After that Supercool,
Then Eternal Refrigeration."

—*Anonymous*

GENTOO PENGUINS

Anemone

A flower with no smell,
A fisher with no line,
A trapper with no lure
Who, mouthless, still can dine.

A rider without legs,
A killer without hands
Who, silent, waits a lifetime
On shifting sea-soft sands.

—*Jane Yolen*

FISH-EATING ANEMONE

The **Starfish**

When I see a starfish
Upon the shining sand,
I ask him how he liked the sea
And if he likes the land.
"Would you rather be a starfish
Or an out-beyond-the-bar fish?"
I whisper very softly,
And he seems to understand.

He never *says* directly,
But I fancy all the same
That he knows the answer quite as well
As if it were his name:
"An out-beyond-the-bar fish
Is much happier than a starfish";
And when I look for him again
He's gone the way he came.

—David McCord

SEAL

See how he dives
  From the rocks with a zoom!
  See how he darts
    Through his watery room
    Past crabs and eels
    And green seaweed,
    Past fluffs of sandy
    Minnow feed!
    See how he swims
    With a swerve and a twist,
  A flip of the flipper,
  A flick of the wrist!
  Quicksilver-quick,
 Softer than spray,
Down he plunges
And sweeps away;
Before you can think,
Before you can utter
 Words like "Dill pickle"
  Or "Apple butter,"
  Back up he swims
    Past Sting Ray and Shark,
    Out with a zoom,
    A whoop, a bark;
    Before you can say
      Whatever you wish,
      He plops at your side
      With a mouthful of fish!

—*William Jay Smith*

The Performing Seal

Who is so proud
As not to feel
A secret awe
Before a seal
That keeps such sleek
And wet repose
While twirling candles
On his nose?

—Rachel Field

Seal Lullaby

Oh! hush thee, my baby, the night is behind us,
And black are the waters that sparkled so green.
The moon, o'er the combers, looks downward to find us
At rest in the hollows that rustle between.
Where billow meets billow, there soft be thy pillow;
Ah, weary wee flipperling, curl at thy ease!
The storm shall not wake thee, nor sharks overtake thee,
Asleep in the arms of the slow-swinging seas.

—Rudyard Kipling

CRABEATER SEAL

The Walrus

The widdly, waddly walrus
has flippery, floppery feet.
He dives in the ocean for dinner
and stands on his noggin to eat.

The wrinkly, crinkly walrus
swims with a debonair splash.
His elegant tusks are of ivory
and he wears a fine walrus moustache.

The thundery, blundery walrus
has a rubbery, blubbery hide.
He puffs up his neck when it's bedtime
and floats fast asleep on the tide.

—Jack Prelutsky

The Eel

I don't mind eels
Except as meals
And the way they feels.

—Ogden Nash

GARDEN EEL

WALRUS

Beavers in November

This stick   here
That stick   there
   Mud, more mud, add mud, good mud
That stick   here
This stick   there
   Mud, more mud, add mud, good mud
     You pat
     I gnaw
     I pile
     You store
This stick   here
That stick   there
   Mud, more mud, add mud, good mud

     You guard
     I pack
     I dig
     You stack
That stick   here
This stick   there
   Mud, more mud, add mud, good mud
     I trim
     You mold
     To keep
     Out cold
This stick   here
That stick   there
   Mud, more mud, add mud, good mud

—*Marilyn Singer*

NORTH AMERICAN BEAVER

There Was an
Old Person of Hyde

There was an old person of Hyde,
Who walked by the shore with his bride,
Till a Crab who came near, fill'd their bosoms with fear,
And they said, "Would we'd never left Hyde!"

—*Edward Lear*

Young Prince Pinch

Young Prince Pinch
was a jolly young prince
and a jolly young prince was he.
He sharpened his claws
and he sharpened his jaws
and he sharpened his pincers on me!

—*Avis Harley*

The Crab

Don't ever grab
old crusty crab
because
with all those claws
he'll maybe grab you first
and you'll come off the worst!
I knew a small boy long ago
o long and long and long ago
whose mother said she did not know
just where the crab's eyes were: and so
he pointed with his finger, and
that crab politely took his hand
as if to say let's take a walk
and have a talk
upon this lovely seaside wharf:
and had to be flung off:
but on his finger left a dent
that lasted days before it went.
He doesn't sing he isn't mean
in fact he keeps the water clean
by eating up the scraps galore
that litter up the ocean's floor:
and if at times he can be vicious
remember he is so nutritious
and O in soups delicious!
(Perhaps it's mean
to mention a tureen.)
Old crusty crab, all claws no head,
he scuttles on the ocean bed
but never said
or so I've heard
a single crusty
or crustacean
word.

—*Conrad Aiken*

Happy the Ocean

Angry the ocean
In hurricane season

Peaceful the ocean
Its whitecaps napping

Gloomy the ocean
As sky mirrors darken

Sunny the ocean
Yacht riggings snapping

Blue-green the ocean
In deep-shallow waters

Moody the ocean
Gone mad in a minute

Busy the ocean
With cargo and cruises

Happy the ocean
With dolphins in it

—Anonymous

BOTTLENOSE DOLPHINS

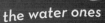

Sea Turtle

Inquisitive, she surveys the blue-black wilderness.
Alone, she seeks peace in the waving sargassum.
Noble, she spurns the long nets and the soup pots
   of greedy nations.
Driven, she navigates her island night landing
   to returtle the sea.
Fulfilled, she does not wait for the brash hatchling
   dash to the wall of gulls.
At eighty, she has seen enough of the wide wet world
   and is content with letting go.

                              —*Anonymous*

Turtles

Turtles sit.
Turtles wait.
Turtles never
Think they're late.

Turtles crawl.
Turtles snap.
Turtles take
A long, long nap.

Turtles listen.
Turtles hide.
Turtles like
To stay inside.

                              —*Charles Ghigna*

GREEN SEA TURTLE

The Shark

A treacherous monster is the Shark
He never makes the least remark.
And when he sees you on the sand,
He doesn't seem to want to land.
He watches you take off your clothes,
And not the least excitement shows.
His eyes do not grow bright or roll,
He has astonishing self-control.
He waits till you are quite undressed,
And seems to take no interest.
And when towards the sea you leap,
He looks as if he were asleep.
But when you once get in his range,
His whole demeanor seems to change.
He throws his body right about,
And his true character comes out.
It's no use crying or appealing,
He seems to lose all decent feeling.
After this warning you will wish
To keep clear of this treacherous fish.
His back is black, his stomach white,
He has a very dangerous bite.

—Lord Alfred Douglas

About the
Teeth of
Sharks

The thing about shark teeth is—teeth,
One row above, one row beneath.

Now take a close look. Do you find
It has another row behind?

Still closer—here, I'll hold your hat:
Has it a third row behind that?

Now look in and . . . Look out! Oh my,
I'll *never* know now! Well, goodbye.

—*John Ciardi*

CARIBBEAN REEF SHARK

Sea Jelly

It's not made of jelly; it isn't a fish.
Mostly it drifts, but can move with a swish.
It doesn't have lungs or a brain; most can't see.
It captures its dinner tentacularly.
Named after a Gorgon who turned men to stone,
It's best if you leave this Medusa alone.

—*Kelly Ramsdell Fineman*

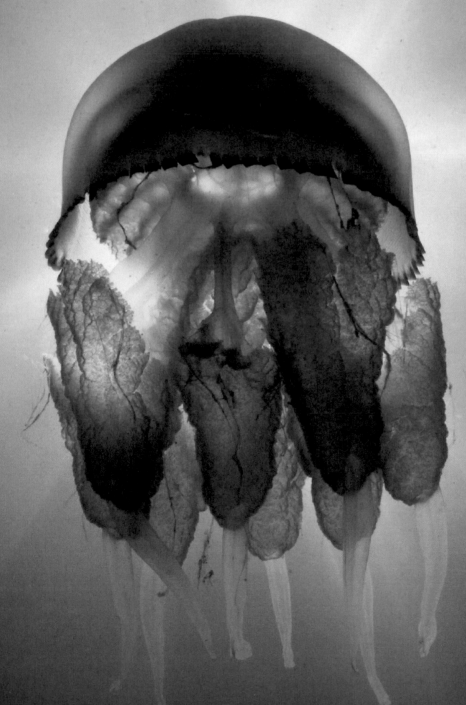

BARREL JELLYFISH

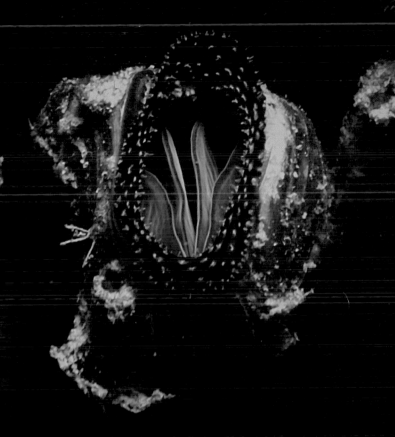

Do Oysters Sneeze?

Do oysters sneeze beneath the seas,
or wiggle to and fro,
or sulk, or smile, or dance awhile
. . . how can we ever know?

Do oysters yawn when roused at dawn,
and do they ever weep,
and can we tell, when in its shell,
an oyster is asleep?

—*Jack Prelutsky*

Mussel

One valve, two valve,
Mollusk, mussel,
Shells itself from
Hustle, bustle.
Keeping still is
No impediment.
Buried under
Muddy sediment.

But when it tires
Of life's low lull,
It hitches to
A tanker's hull
And rides the trade routes
While it can
From Kowloon Bay
North to Japan.

—*Steven Withrow*

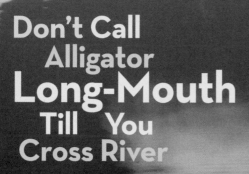

Don't Call
Alligator
Long-Mouth
Till You
Cross River

Call alligator long-mouth
call alligator saw-mouth
call alligator pushy-mouth
call alligator scissors-mouth
call alligator raggedy-mouth
call alligator bumpy-bum
call alligator all dem rude word
      but better wait
      till you cross river.

     —John Agard

The Crocodile

How doth the little crocodile
    Improve his shining tail,
And pour the waters of the Nile
    On every golden scale!

How cheerfully he seems to grin,
    How neatly spreads his claws,
And welcomes little fishes in,
    With gently smiling jaws!

—*Lewis Carroll*

Dark Meat

Once I had a crocodile
    For a pet.
Unfortunately, no one's
    Found me yet.

—*Anonymous*

CROCODILE

THE STRANGE ONES

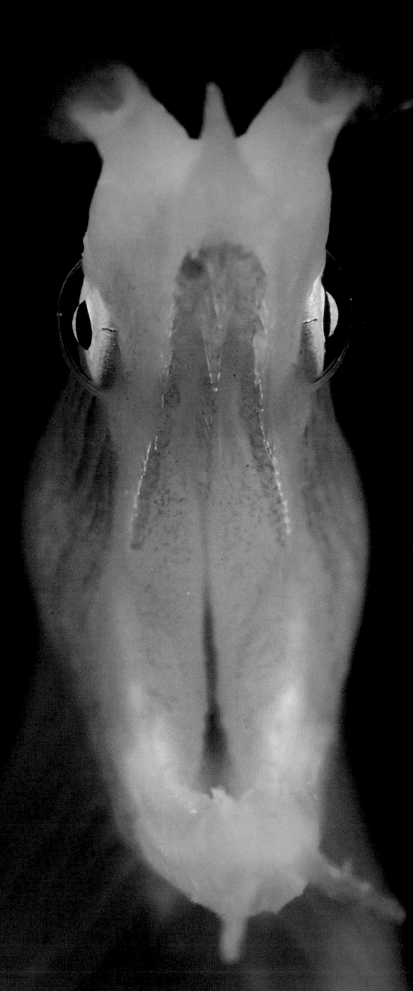

Moray EEL

Nighttime's my bright time.
It's head-out-and-bite time.
Give-shellfish-a-fright time.
Swim-quick-as-a-kite time.
Stay-out-of-my-sight time.
Or fins-up-and-fight time.
When I am the blight of the sea.

It's switch-on-the-light time.
Height-of-my-might time.
Turn-mollusks-all-white time.
And wrap-them-up-tight time.
No-care-for-their-plight time.
Yes, nighttime's my bright time.
Oh, nighttime's the right time for me!

—*Steven Withrow*

All You Oughta Know About a Piranha

All you wanna know about a piranha
is . . . you don't wanna know a piranha.

And, if ever you needta meet a piranha,
you needta keep in mind: you're meat.

—Michael J. Rosen

The Ostrich

The ostrich roams the great Sahara.
Its mouth is wide, its neck is narra.
It has such long and lofty legs,
I'm glad it sits to lay its eggs.

—Ogden Nash

The Ostrich
Is a Silly
Bird

The ostrich is a silly bird,
   With scarcely any mind.
He often runs so very fast,
   He leaves himself behind,

And when he gets there, has to stand
   And hang about till night,
Without a blessed thing to do
   Until he comes in sight.

—Mary E. Wilkins Freeman

I Am a Baby Porcupette

I am a baby porcupette.
My paws are small; my nose is wet.
And as I nurse against my mom,
we mew and coo a soft duet.

I am a baby porcupette.
I cannot climb up branches yet.
While Mom sleeps in the trees, I curl
beneath a log till sun has set.

I am a baby porcupette.
I nibble in the nighttime wet:
a sprig of leaves, a tuft of grass,
in hidden spots I won't forget.

I am a baby porcupette.
My fur is soft; my eyes are jet.
But I can deal with any threat:
I raise my quills
              and pirouette.

—Joyce Sidman

Porcupine

Bedazzled by bristles,
bewhiskered with points,
lumbering
on clumsy joints—
shuffling along
knobby branch of pine;
rattling quills
    along his spine,
he nestles into
branch of chair,
settles down
to evening air—
tightly tucked
and in between
shade of spruce;
sweet evergreen,

quiet prince of timber, he
needles into limb
and tree;
claims this place—
ah, forest throne,
to wind and woodlands
    he calls home.

—Rebecca Kai Dotlich

The Octopus

Tell me, O Octopus, I begs
Is those things arms,
or is they legs?
I marvel at thee,
Octopus;
If I were thou, I'd call me Us.

—*Ogden Nash*

DAY OCTOPUS

Seahorse

O under the ocean waves
I gallop the seaweed lanes,
I jump the coral reef,
And all with no saddle or reins.

I haven't a flowing mane,
I've only this horsy face,
But under the ocean waves
I'm king of the steeplechase.

—Blake Morrison

What Is the
Opposite of
Pillow?

What is the opposite of *pillow*?
The answer, child, is *armadillo*.
"Oh, don't talk nonsense!" you protest.
However, if you tried to rest
Your head upon the creature, you
Would find that what I say is true.
It isn't soft. From head to tail
It wears a scratchy coat of mail.

And furthermore, it won't hold still
Upon a bed, as pillows will,
But squirms, and jumps at every chance
To run away and eat some ants.

So there! Admit that I was right,
Or else we'll have a *pillow fight*.

—*Richard Wilbur*

NINE-BANDED ARMADILLO

The **Anteater**

The
 anteater's
  long
   and
   tacky
    tongue
     is
     snaking
      from
      its
       snout.

A thousand termites riding in,
But no one riding out.

—*Douglas Florian*

The **Argument**

The aardvark and the armadillo
can't decide which tastes the best.
"An anthill!" says the armadillo.
Aardvark insists, "A termite nest!"

—*Bobbi Katz*

GIANT ANTEATER

Travel Plans

If I could go anywhere,
    here's what I'd do.
I'd pop in the pouch of a kind
    kangaroo.
I'd travel around for as long
    as I pleased,
And learn to say "thank you"
    in Kangarooese.

—*Bobbi Katz*

RED KANGAROO

The Meerkats of Africa

Meerkats go about in packs,
They don't hang loose—
They're not really *cats* at all,
But more a mongoose.
They have great capabilities,
Make no mistake,
A Meerkat can kill a scorpion
Or even a snake.
They rescue each other's children
And have lookouts when they're feeding
And a system of babysitters—
The kind of co-operation
That the human race is needing!

—*Gavin Ewart*

MEERKATS

Sand Ghost

stingray resting
in the ocean sand
you're camouflaged
brown on tan,
then like a ghost
you rise and hover,
like a billow of brown
rippling around,
your arms spread wide
you glide and flap
then hide again
and disappear
were you ever here?

—Betsy Franco

ATLANTIC STINGRAY

Frilled
Lizard

Expansion Collar
Instructions for Operation

When not in use, the collar hangs
in compact folds of skin
conveniently tucked away
beneath the wearer's chin.

Activate the collar by
inflation of the lungs,
full extension of the jaws,
projection of the tongue.

Discourages a predator
two times out of three.
Batteries are not required.

Lifetime guarantee.

—Alice Schertle

The Yak

As a friend to the children
  commend me the Yak.
   You will find it exactly the thing:
It will carry and fetch,
  you can ride on its back,
Or lead it about
  with a string.
The Tartar who dwells on the plains of Thibet
  (A desolate region of snow)
Has for centuries made it a nursery pet,
  And surely the Tartar should know!
Then tell your papa where the Yak can be got,
  And if he is awfully rich
He will buy you the creature—
  or else
      he will *not*.
(I cannot be positive which.)

—*Hilaire Belloc*

YAK

How to Tell a Camel

The **D**romedary has one hump,
The **B**actrian has two.

It's easy to forget this rule,
So here is what to do.
Roll the first initial over
On its flat behind:

The **DB**actrian is different from
The **DB**romedary kind.

—*J. Patrick Lewis*

BACTRIAN CAMEL

Skunk

Skunk
doesn't slink
but walks the earth
with a sense of worth

and wears with
pride
the bright white
stripe
on his inky
fur.

Skunk won't shrink,
to face a
foe.
Gives fair warning
"Better go!"
and many a foe
has slunk
away.

Skunk is
spunky,
mild as well,
and what a tale his
tail
could tell!

—Lilian Moore

MOLINA'S
HOG-NOSED
SKUNK

A Flamingo Is

A Flamingo
is
a long
coooooooooooooooool
drink
of
something
pink

—J. Patrick Lewis

A
Blue-footed
Booby

You'd never see a bird who'd be
as shod as oddly as the booby.
It struts about on such blue legs
or poses on its clutch of eggs,
sharing baby brooding duties
until they hatch as newbie boobies.

—*Michael J. Rosen*

BLUE-FOOTED BOOBY

Spoonbill
Haiku

The princess of birds.
Her only competition
Is her reflection.

—*Jane Yolen*

How to Paint a Zebra

To paint a zebra, mix the Moon
And Midnight in a can.
Roll it over and under
Shoulder to flank,
Belly to shank—
Midnight & Moon . . .

To zebriate the afternoon.

—*Anonymous*

Zebra

White men in Africa,
Puffing at their pipes,
Think the zebra's a white horse
With black stripes.

Black men in Africa,
With pipes of different types,
Know the zebra's a black horse
With white stripes.

—*Gavin Ewart*

Zebra

white sun
black
fire escape,

morning
grazing like a zebra
outside my window.

—Judith Thurman

A Promise

Zebra, zebra—
wild and free
once you traveled
the African plains.
Caught and caged,
your freedom's gone,
but your wild beauty remains

Zebra, zebra—
one day soon
we'll gallop away
to the sea.
I won't keep you
in a cage.
Together, we both will be
free!

—Bobbi Katz

BURCHELL'S ZEBRAS

A Centipede Was Happy Quite

A centipede was happy quite,
  Until a frog in fun
Said, "Pray, which leg comes after
    which?"
This raised her mind to such a pitch,
She lay distracted in the ditch
  Considering how to run.

—Anonymous

Vanishing Act

Wait.
Is that a wayward dust bunny?
No.
it's the centipede—
a ballet of legs
gliding
skating
skimming
across the stage of white porcelain tile—
vanishing
behind the curtain of stage fright
before I've ever grabbed
a broom.

—Tracie Vaughn Zimmer

Proboscis Monkey Ponders Man

The creature does nothing
but stand and stare.
Nobody knows
what he's doing there,
prowling the Primate Habitat,
finding someone
to ogle at.
Nobody knows
what he hopes to see,
gawking, squawking,
staring at me . . .
   Ha!
   Ha!
   Ha!
Tedious call.
His brain,
like his nose,
is probably
small.

—Alice Schertle

PROBOSCIS MONKEY

THE NOISY ONES

CRAB-EATING MACAQUE

The Frog

Be kind and tender to the Frog,
  And do not call him names,
As "Slimy-Skin," or "Polly-wog,"
  Or likewise, "Ugly James,"
Or "Gape-a-grin," or "Toad-gone-
    wrong,"
  Or "Billy-Bandy-knees";
The Frog is justly sensitive
  To epithets like these.

No animal will more repay
  A treatment kind and fair,
At least, so lonely people say
Who keep a frog (and, by the way,
  They are extremely rare).

—*Hilaire Belloc*

FROG   AMERICAN BULLFROG

The **BULL**

Do they watch me trot to the top of the hill,
the cows who are milling and mooing?
　　I bellow and blow and paw the ground
　　and make a sort of a snorting sound
　　and toss my terrible horns around—
(*The cows—have they stopped their chewing?*)

I'm striking a pose; I'm standing still
as a statue here on the top of the hill.
　　I flick my tail, as I stately stand,
　　at a fool of a fly who has dared to land
　　on the royal rump of a bull so grand—
(*Are they watching whatever I'm doing?*)

　　　　　　　　—Alice Schertle

Bull and **Ox**

A *bull* acts like a bully
with a running start.
The ox enjoys a pull. He
tows any plow or cart.
One of them is slow and dull,
both of them are large.
One is unpredictabull—
he's the one in . . .

　　　　　c h a r g e!

　　　　　　　　—*Anonymous*

Crickets

they   tell
the   time
of   night
they   tick

the   time
of   night
they   tick
they   tell

of   night
they   tick
and   tell
the   time

they   tick
they   tell
the   time
they   click

—*Myra Cohn Livingston*

Splinter

The voice of the last cricket
across the first frost
is one kind of good-bye.
It is so thin a splinter of singing.

—Carl Sandburg

Crickets

We cannot say that crickets sing
Since all they do is twang a wing.

Especially when the wind is still
They orchestrate a sunlit hill.

And in the evening blue above
They weave the stars and moon with love.

Then peacefully they chirp all night
Remembering delight, delight . . .

—Harry Behn

Why Pigs Cannot Write Poems

Pigs cannot write poems because
Nothing rhymes with *oink*. If you
Think you can find a rhyme, I'll pause,
But if I wait until you do,
I'll have forgotten why it was
Pigs cannot write poems because.

—John Ciardi

Pig

Pig, pig,
What have you brought me?

—Mud and a grunt and an oink.

Pig, pig,
What can I do
With mud and a grunt and an oink?

—With mud, said the pig,
You can wallow and play,
With a grunt, said the pig,
You can snooze all day,
With an oink, said the pig . . .
Then it dozed away.

So what can I do with this oink, I say,
What can I do with this oink?

—Richard Edwards

Summertime

Was ever a pig
contented as this,
to roll in the mud
and know the bliss
of cooling off
in the muck
and grime,
having the grubbiest
mussiest
time?

and then, when he's cool,
to slowly rise
and dry himself off
in the summer skies,
and sniff for his supper
and slop up his feed—
What else
does a happy
piggy
need?

—*Myra Cohn Livingston*

Piety

The pig is taught by sermons and epistles
To think the God of Swine has snout and bristles.

—*Ambrose Bierce*

Dog

The sky is the belly of a large dog,
sleeping.
All day the small gray flag of his ear
is lowered and raised.
The dream he dreams has no beginning.

Here on earth we dream
a deep-eyed dog sleeps under our stairs
and will rise to meet us.
Dogs curl in dark places,
nests of rich leaves.
We want to bury ourselves
in someone else's home.

The dog who floats over us
has no master.
If there were people who loved him,
he remembers them equally,
the one who smelled like smoke,
the one who brought bones from the restaurant.
It is the long fence
of their hoping he would stay
that he has jumped.

—*Naomi Shihab Nye*

Unpopular
Rex

When our hound dog Rex
   Picked a fight with a skunk
It took ten weeks
   Till his atmosphere shrunk.

All that terrible while,
   Drooping tail, he fretted—
Why do they yell, he wondered,
   When I want to be petted?

—*X. J. Kennedy*

The **Breed You Need**

If the dog you want has a pedigree,
Then the dog you want simply won't be me.
My crisscrossed bloodlines could derail a train
So the kennel club treats me with disdain.
Are you someone who loves a mystery?
Consider the clues; unlatch my history!
I've the best of this and the best of that
And "pedigree" soon will be so old hat.

If you want a dog with a heart that's true,
Then I am the dog who is meant for you.
The breed you need is spelled M-U-T-T.
I'm a marvelous mutt, so please choose me.

—*Bobbi Katz*

The Greater Cats

The greater cats with golden eyes
Stare out between the bars.
Deserts are there, and different skies,
And night with different stars.

—V. Sackville-West

You've Got Male

Lion prowls through his jungle domain
looking proud as a peacock, and vain.
  He's so macho-superb
  he has earned his own verb.
How we *lionize* such a great mane!

—Avis Harley

Lion

Tiredness
gets caught in your throat.

Lion casts it out with a fierce exhale,
mouth wide open,
and lets it roll off his tongue.

—Janet S. Wong

AFRICAN LIONS

136

A Picture of the Rooster

A crimson comb untrimmed on the head,
All in white, a rooster walks nearby.
In his life seldom a single sound he's made,
But thousands of doors soon open to his cry.

—*Tang Yin*

Raccoon

This cartoon bandit
rubs hands together, ready
for a midnight crime.

—*Janet S. Wong*

from Road-Song of the Bandar-Log

Here we sit in a branchy row,
Thinking of beautiful things we know;
Dreaming of deeds that we mean to do,
All complete, in a minute or two—
Something noble and grand and good,
Won by merely wishing we could.
    Now we're going to—never mind,
    Brother, thy tail hangs down behind!

All the talk we ever have heard
Uttered by bat or beast or bird—
Hide or fin or scale or feather—
Jabber it quickly and all together!
Excellent! Wonderful! Once again!
Now we are talking just like men.
    Let's pretend we are . . . Never mind,
    Brother, thy tail hangs down behind!
    This is the way of the Monkey-kind.

        —Rudyard Kipling

SQUIRREL MONKEY

from **The Law of the Jungle**

Now this is the Law of the Jungle—as old and as true as the sky;
And the Wolf that shall keep it may prosper, but the Wolf that shall break it must die.
As the creeper that girdles the tree-trunk the Law runneth forward and back—
For the strength of the Pack is the Wolf, and the strength of the Wolf is the Pack.

—Rudyard Kipling

Why Wolves **Howl**

Gray wolves do not howl at the moon.
Across a vast
timber
zone,
they oboe in
mono-
tone,
Fur-face, I am
all a-
lone.

—*Anonymous*

GRAY WOLF

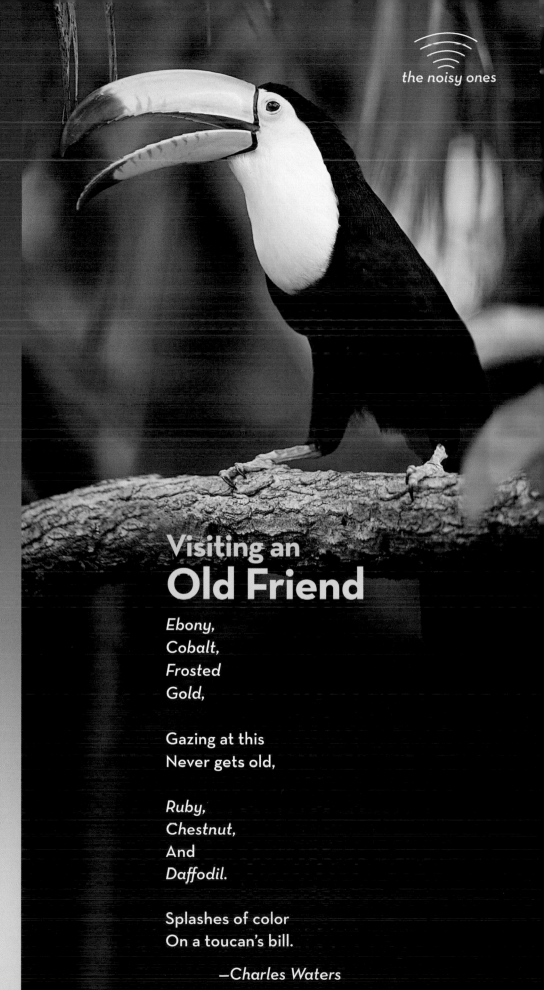

Jack A.

The donkey is an ani-mule
Who won't put up with ridi-cule.
His temper's short and, as a rule,
He's seldom very tame.

Especially, if he's called Old Zack
Or Shorty Horse or Prickleback.
And if, of course, you call him Jack,
Don't mention his last name.

—*J. Patrick Lewis*

The Donkey

Donkey, donkey, old and gray,
Open your mouth and gently bray;
Lift your ears and blow your horn,
To wake the world this sleepy morn.

—*A nursery rhyme*

Visiting an Old Friend

Ebony,
Cobalt,
Frosted
Gold,

Gazing at this
Never gets old,

Ruby,
Chestnut,
And
Daffodil.

Splashes of color
On a toucan's bill.

—*Charles Waters*

KEEL-BILLED TOUCAN

THE QUIET ONES

Rabbit

A rabbit
bit
A little bit
An itty-bitty
Little bit of beet.
Then bit
By bit
He bit
Because he liked the taste of it.
But when he bit
A wee bit more,
It was more bitter than before.
"This beet is bitter!"
Rabbit cried.
"I feel a bit unwell inside!"
But when he bit
Another bite, that bit of beet
Seemed quite all right.
Besides
When all is said and done,
Better bitter beet
Than none.

—Mary Ann Hoberman

COTTONTAIL RABBIT

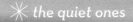

Four Ducks
on a Pond

Four ducks on a pond,
A grass-bank beyond,
A blue sky of spring,
White clouds on the wing;
What a little thing
To remember for years—
To remember with tears!

—*William Allingham*

MALLARD DUCKLINGS

Firefly

A Song

A little light is going by,
Is going up to see the sky,
A little light with wings.

I never could have thought of it,
To have a little bug all lit
And made to go on wings.

—*Elizabeth Madox Roberts*

Luna Moth

Out of a windless August night,
A luna moth in ghostly light

Beat softly on my window screen—
Tick-tick-ticking—all silver-green.

She whispered secrets in my ear—
I am but a stranger here.

*The stars are scrawled across the sky
By ghostwriters, the Moon and I.*

*You will not see me here tonight—
I have a thousand stars to write.*

—J. Patrick Lewis

The Warning

Just now,
Out of the strange
Still dusk . . . as strange as still . . .
A white moth flew.
Why am I grown so cold?

—Adelaide Crapsey

Home to **Roost**

The chickens
are circling and
blotting out the
day. The sun is
bright, but the
chickens are in
the way. Yes,
the sky is dark
with chickens,
dense with them.
They turn and
then they turn
again. These
are the chickens
you let loose
one at a time
and small—
various breeds.
Now they have
come home
to roost—all
the same kind
at the same speed.

—*Kay Ryan*

CHICKENS

The Hens

The night was coming very fast;
It reached the gate as I ran past.

The pigeons had gone to the tower of the church
And all the hens were on their perch,

Up in the barn, and I thought I heard
A piece of a little purring word.

I stopped inside, waiting and staying,
To try to hear what the hens were saying.

They were asking something, that was plain,
Asking it over and over again.

One of them moved and turned around,
Her feathers made a ruffled sound,

A ruffled sound, like a bushful of birds,
And she said her little asking words.

She pushed her head close into her wing,
But nothing answered anything.

—*Elizabeth Madox Roberts*

Haiku

The chicken scratching
for food in the dirt stirs up
tiny tornados.

—*Kristine O'Connell George*

Cat in the Snow

Stepping gingerly,
he goes
through the garden
when it snows,
hoping not
to wet his toes.
And I'm sure
he never knows
every footprint
is a rose.

—*Aileen Fisher*

Fog

The fog comes
on little cat feet.

It sits looking
over harbor and city
on silent haunches
and then moves on.

—*Carl Sandburg*

Haiku

Cat preens in the sun,
smoothing her ruffled fur robe.
The fleas are awake.

—*Avis Harley*

Two Cats

There once were two cats of Kilkenny,
Each thought there was one cat too many;
    So they fought and they fit,
    And they scratched and they bit,
Till instead of two cats there weren't any.

—*Anonymous*

DOMESTIC CAT

Sunning

Old Dog lay in the summer sun
Much too lazy to rise and run.
He flapped an ear
At a buzzing fly.
He winked a half opened
Sleepy eye.
He scratched himself
On an itching spot,
As he dozed on the porch
Where the sun was hot.
He whimpered a bit
From force of habit
While he lazily dreamed
Of chasing a rabbit.
But Old Dog happily lay in the sun
Much too lazy to rise and run.

—*James S. Tippett*

Pet Snake

No trace of fuzz.

No bit of fur.

No growling bark,

or gentle purr.

No cozy cuddle.

No sloppy kiss.

All he really does

is hissssssssss.

—Rebecca Kai Dotlich

Dressing Like a Snake

A snake changes its clothes
only twice a year.
Beginning with its nose,
peeling down to its toes:
new clothes suddenly appear.
Wouldn't it be nice
to dress only twice
instead of each day of the year?

—Georgia Heard

Snake

The word begins to
hiss as soon as the first
letter
goes on   S
s-s-s-s-s-s   forked tongue flickers
Hard eyes stare
Already the rest of the poem
shrinks back from
his narrow speed   The paper
draws in its breath   S N A K E
loops around the pencil
slides
among typewriter keys   slips
like a silk shoelace
away

—Barbara Juster Esbensen

GOPHER SNAKE

The Panther

The panther is like a leopard,
Except it hasn't been peppered.
Should you behold a panther crouch,
Prepare to say Ouch.
Better yet, if called by a panther,
Don't anther.

—Ogden Nash

BLACK JAGUAR

Coyote
Landscape

For a moment, you are as still
As the roots, rocks, snow.
Only the water runs fast,
As fast as you, when you go

Whipping the wind, blazing the trail,
Following the panting prey.
But now, for a moment, you stand statue still
Reflecting on the day.

—Jane Yolen

I Saw a Sloth Play Soccer

I saw a sloth play soccer
with a tortoise and a snail.
They were all enthusiastic
and determined to prevail.

They were positively passionate
and truly in the groove,
and by watching very closely
I could almost see them move.

—Kenn Nesbitt

THREE-TOED SLOTH

from I Have Lived &
and I Have Loved

I have lived and I have loved;
I have waked and I have slept;
I have sung and I have danced;
I have smiled and I have wept;
I have won and wasted treasure;
I have had my fill of pleasure;
And all these things were weariness,
And some of them were dreariness.
And all these things—but two things
Were emptiness and pain:
And Love—it was the best of them;
And Sleep—worth all the rest of them.

—Charles Mackay

TABBY CAT

"I Am Home,"
Said the Turtle

"I am home," said the turtle, as it pulled in its head
And its feet, and its tail. "I am home, and in bed.

"No matter what inches and inches I roam,
When the long day is done, I am always at home.

"I may go whole feet . . . even yards . . . in a day,
But I never get lost, for I'm never away

"From my snug little house and my snug little bed.
Try being a turtle!—That's using your head!

"You can go on forever, no matter how far,
And whatever you need is wherever you are!"

("Is there one thing I miss when I'm snuggled in tight?
Yes: there's no room for someone to kiss me good night.")

—John Ciardi

YELLOW-SPOTTED AMAZON RIVER TURTLE

Box Turtle

A hummock of stone lapped in wrinkles; four tiny
tree trunks sprouting claws. A cup on top of a plate.
And in that soft space between, dusty wattles of
skin. Breath like old leaves. Tail that is hardly there.
A hooked, patrician nose. Broad bridge of brow
daubed in gold, and beneath it: one cranberry eye,
fixed on me, glittering.

—*Joyce Sidman*

The Tortoise

I am a tortoise,
slow and sure,
close to the earth
that I adore,

close enough
to feel the beat,
of buried rivers
beneath my feet.

I am a quiet,
steady poem—
my shell protects me
as I roam,

shelters me from
nature's wrath,
as I walk
my dusty path.

—*Joan Bransfield Graham*

163

FINAL

Animals

I think I could turn and live with animals, they are so
placid and self-contain'd;
I stand and look at them long and long.
They do not sweat and whine about their condition;
They do not lie awake in the dark and weep for their sins;
They do not make me sick discussing their duty to God;
Not one is dissatisfied—not one is demented with the mania
   of owning things;
Not one kneels to another, nor to his kind that lived
   thousands of years ago;
Not one is respectable or industrious over the whole earth.

—*Walt Whitman*

AFRICAN LEOPARD

THOUGHT

Hurt No Living Thing

Hurt no living thing;
Ladybird, nor butterfly,
Nor moth with dusty wing,
Nor cricket chirping cheerily,
Nor grasshopper so light of leap,
Nor dancing gnat, nor beetle fat,
Nor harmless worms that creep.

—*Christina Georgina Rossetti*

Magic Words

In the very earliest time,
when both people and animals lived on earth,
a person could become an animal if he wanted to
and an animal could become a human being.
Sometimes they were people
and sometimes animals
and there was no difference.
All spoke the same language.
That was the time when words were like magic.
The human mind had mysterious powers.
A word spoken by chance
might have strange consequences.
It would suddenly come alive
and what people wanted to happen could happen.
Nobody could explain this:
That's the way it was.

—An Inuit poem, translated
by Edward Field

AFRICAN ELEPHANT

Make the Earth
Your Companion

Make the Earth your companion.
    Walk lightly on it, as other creatures do.
Let the Sky paint her beauty—she is always
    watching over you.
Learn from the Sea how to face harsh forces.
Let the River remind you that everything will pass.
Let the Lake instruct you in stillness.
Let the Mountain teach you grandeur.
Make the Woodland your house of peace.
Make the Rainforest your house of hope.
Meet the Wetland on twilight ground.
Save some small piece of Grassland for a red kite
    on a windy day.
Watch the Icecaps glisten with crystal majesty.
Hear the Desert whisper hush to eternity.
Let the Town weave a small basket of togetherness.
Make the Earth your companion.
    Walk lightly on it, as other creatures do.

—J. Patrick Lewis

writing poems
about animals

Writing poems about animals can be fun and rewarding, but also challenging. The best way to start is **not** to state the obvious, but as Emily Dickinson once said, "Tell all the truth but tell it slant."

> Is that spring winging
> into the backyard, ready
> to play tug-of-worm?

Did you guess this was a poem about a robin? Correct!

Go ahead, challenge yourself. Try to describe a zebra without using the words "black," "white," or "striped." Don't worry about rhyming. Rhyming is serious business (if it is to be done well). It's not just one of your holiday games. For now, just think about how you can best describe a zebra without sounding like the dictionary or an encyclopedia.

If you are feeling adventurous, then try experimenting with different forms of poetry:

COUPLET
is a pair of lines of verse, especially a pair that rhymes and whose lines are about the same length.

Trail Mix

Who is a happy rabbit owner? Well, it's
A kid who happens to be fond of pellets.

SHAPE POEM
Its name tells you exactly what it is.

A Flamingo
i
s

a

l
o
n
g
cooooooooooboooooool
d r i n k
o
f
s p
o i
m n
e k
t
h
i
n
g

HAIKU
Like the "robin" poem above, a haiku is a three-line poem of 5-7-5 syllables that describes something in nature. Actually, most modern haiku poets

experiment with fewer than 17 syllables, like the poem below. It's okay to break the rules once you know them.

> An otter water-
> toboggans down
> the backside of life

LIMERICK
is a witty, five-line poem that rhymes AABBA and has a da-DUM da-da DUM da-da DUM rhythm:

How the Rhinoceros Got His Nose

The very first Rhino (from Tokyo)
Just loved telling joke after jokeo,
   But he also told lies
   Of incredible size,
Which is how he became a Rhinocchio.

FREE VERSE
is a poetic form that does not use strict rhyme and meter:

Alone in Winter

Have you come upon a doe,
   alone in winter?
I did once. She was shy.
Wind galloped through the trees
and the trees stepped back
and the doe made a slow
circle in the air
with her wet black nose,
as if to say,
I have come upon a boy,
   alone in winter.

There are many forms available to the poet, so pick one that looks inviting.

Here are a few other ideas for getting started:

1. An animal can't talk back to you, but you can talk (write) to it, and what you have to say is called an apostrophe poem. Pick an animal (or any object) and tell him or her or it what you are thinking.

2. Pretend you <u>are</u> an animal. What would your life be like if you were a giraffe, a hippo, a mouse? Poets call this a mask poem, because you are pretending to be that animal by wearing its mask.

3. Try a cinquain, a five-line poem, starting with 2, then 4, 6, 8, and 2 syllables in each successive line.

4. Write a poem in two voices: you and your sister, or you and a best friend.

Keep in mind what Robert Frost once wrote: "All the fun's in how you say a thing."

SCARLET IBIS

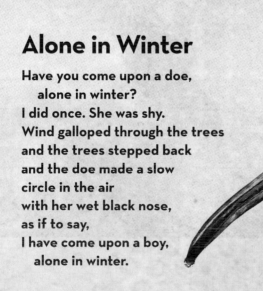

171

resources

Here is a selected bibliography of children's books on wordplay that you might find especially useful as you explore your own paths to poetry.

ACROSTICS

Harley, Avis. *African Acrostics: A Word in Edgeways.* Candlewick, 2009.

Schnur, Steven. *Autumn: An Alphabet Acrostic.* Clarion, 1997. (See also his *Winter, Spring,* and *Summer* acrostic books in this series.)

ANAGRAMS

Lederer, Richard. *The Circus of Words.* Chicago Review Press, 2001.

Raczka, Bob. *Lemonade: and Other Poems Squeezed from a Single Word.* Roaring Brook, 2011.

DOUBLE DACTYLS, OR IF YOU PREFER, HIGGLEDY-PIGGLEDYS

Hecht Anthony, and John Hollander, eds. *Jiggery Pokery: A Compendium of Double Dactyls.* Atheneum, 1967.

EPITAPHS

Lewis, J. Patrick. *Once Upon a Tomb: Gravely Humorous Verses.* Candlewick, 2006.

Lewis, J. Patrick, and Jane Yolen. *Last Laughs: Animal Epitaphs.* Charlesbridge, 2012.

LIPOGRAMS

Lawson, JonArno. *A Voweller's Bestiary.* Porcupine's Quill, 2008.

LITTLE WILLIES

Invented by Harry Graham, showcased by X. J. Kennedy in his *Brats* books.

PALINDROMES

Agee, Jon. *Go, Hang a Salami! I'm a Lasagna Hog! And Other Palindromes.* Farrar, Straus, Giroux, 1994. (See also the other books in the series.)

PARODIES

Shapiro, Karen Jo. *I Must Go Down to the Beach Again.* Charlesbridge, 2007.

Sidman, Joyce. *This Is Just to Say.* Houghton Mifflin, 2007.

PORTMANTEAUS

Prelutsky, Jack. *Scranimals.* HarperCollins, 2002.

——. *Behold the Bold Umbrellaphant.* Greenwillow, 2006.

REBUSES

Calmenson, Stephanie. *Kindergarten Kids: Riddles, Rebuses, Wiggles, Giggles, and More!* HarperCollins, 2005.

Lewis, J. Patrick. *The Fantastic 5&10 Cent Store.* Schwartz and Wade/Random House, 2010.

REVERSOS

Singer, Marilyn. *Mirror, Mirror.* Dutton, 2010.

SHAPED POEMS

Franco, Betsy. *A Curious Collection of Cats.* Tricycle Press, 2009.

Graham, Joan Bransfield. *Splish Splash.* Houghton Mifflin, 2001.

——. *Flicker Flash.* Houghton Mifflin, 2003.

Grandits, John. *Technically, It's Not My Fault.* Sandpiper, 2004.

——. *Blue Lipstick: Concrete Poems.* Clarion Books, 2007.

Janeczko, Paul B., ed. *A Poke in the I.* Candlewick Press, 2001.

Lewis, J. Patrick. *Doodle Dandies.* Atheneum, 1998.

Magee, Wes, ed. *Madtail, Miniwhale and Other Shape Poems.* Puffin, 1989.

Roemer, Heidi. *Come to My Party and Other Shape Poems.* Henry Holt, 2004.

Joyce Sidman. *Meow Ruff: A Story in Concrete Poetry.* Houghton Mifflin, 2007.

SPOONERISMS

Silverstein, Shel. *Runny Babbitt: A Billy Sook.* HarperCollins, 2005.

TONGUE TWISTERS

Agee, Jon. *Orangutan Tongs.* Hyperion, 2009.

ALL FORMS

Espy, Willard R. *A Children's Almanac of Words at Play.* Clarkson N. Potter, 1982.

Harley, Avis. *Fly with Poetry: An ABC of Poetry.* Wordsong, 2000.

——. *Leap into Poetry: More ABC's of Poetry.* Wordsong, 2001.

Janeczko, Paul B. *A Kick in the Head.* Candlewick, 2005.

——. *Poetry from A to Z: A Guide for Young Writers.* New York: Bradbury, 1994.

Kennedy, X. J., and Dorothy Kennedy. *Knock at a Star: A Child's Introduction to Poetry.* Little, Brown, 1985.

Livingston, Myra Cohn. *Poem-Making: Ways to Begin Writing Poetry.* HarperCollins, 1991.

index

POET INDEX

FIRST LINE INDEX

SUBJECT INDEX

Illustrations are indicated
by **boldface.**

text credits

WELCOME TO THE WORLD

9. **The Egg,** Jack Prelutsky. Used by permission of HarperCollins Publishers.

10. **The Tickle Rhyme,** Ian Serraillier. © Estate of Ian Serraillier.

10. **What's a Caterpillar?,** Graham Denton. "What's a Caterpillar?" previously appeared in *WILD!: Rhymes That Roar*, chosen by James Carter and Graham Denton (Macmillan Children's Books, 2009), and is used with permission of the author.

11. **Cocoon,** David McCord. From *Far and Few* by David McCord. Copyright © 1952 by David McCord. By permission of Little, Brown and Company and the estate of David J. W. McCord. All rights reserved.

13. **Haiku (Jellyfish),** Joan Bransfield Graham. Copyright © 2012 Joan Bransfield Graham. Used by permission of the author, who controls all rights.

THE BIG ONES

17. **Buffalo Dusk,** Carl Sandburg.

18. **Wedding Bears,** J. Patrick Lewis. First published in *Two-Legged, Four-Legged, No-Legged Rhymes*, Knopf, 1991. Copyright © J. Patrick Lewis, 1991.

20. **The Purple Cow,** Gelett Burgess.

20. **Cow,** Valerie Worth. From *All the Small Poems and Fourteen More* by Valerie Worth. Copyright © 1987, 1994 by Valerie Worth. Reprinted by permission of Farrar, Straus and Giroux, LLC.

21. **A Farmer's Boy,** Anonymous.

21. **The Cow,** Robert Louis Stevenson.

21. **The Pasture,** Robert Frost.

23. **Dear Orangutan,** David Elliot. *In the Wild*. Copyright © 2010 by David Elliott. Reproduced by permission of the publisher, Candlewick Press, Somerville, MA.

24. **Moose,** Rebecca Kai Dotlich, Copyright © 2012 by Rebecca Kai Dotlich. Reprinted by permission of Curtis Brown, Ltd.

25. **Song of a Bear,** a Navajo poem.

25. **Grandpa Bear's Lullaby,** Jane Yolen. Copyright © 1981 by Jane Yolen. First appeared in *Dragon Night and Other Lullabies*, published by Methuen. Reprinted by permission of Curtis Brown, Ltd.

26. **Elephant,** Anonymous.

26. **Eletelephony,** Laura E. Richards.

26. **Elephant,** Ann Whitford Paul. By permission of the author, Ann Whitford Paul, 2012.

26. **Anthology,** Tracie Vaughn Zimmer. By permission of the author, Tracie Vaughn Zimmer, 2012.

28. **The Whales Off Wales,** X. J. Kennedy. Copyright © 1975 by X. J. Kennedy. First appeared in *One Winter Night in August*, published by Atheneum. Reprinted by permission of Curtis Brown, Ltd.

29. **Polar Bear Rap,** J. Patrick Lewis. First published in *Countdown to Summer*, 2009. Copyright © J. Patrick Lewis, 2009.

29. **Polar Bear,** Leland Blair Jacobs.

30. **Moody Guy,** Avis Harley. *African Acoustics: A Word in Edgeways.* Copyright © 2009 by Avis Harley. Reproduced by permission of the publisher, Candlewick Press, Somerville, MA.

30. **The White Rhinoceros,** Stephen Mitchell, *The Wishing Bone and Other Poems.* Copyright © 2003 by Stephen Mitchell. Reproduced by permission of the publisher, Candlewick Press, Somerville, MA.

31. **Tiger,** Anonymous.

32. **Giraffe,** Valerie Worth. From *All the Small Poems and Fourteen More* by Valerie Worth. Copyright © 1987, 1994 by Valerie Worth. Reprinted by permission of Farrar, Straus and Giroux, LLC.

32. **Above All,** Avis Harley, *African Acrostics.* Copyright © 2009 by Avis Harley. Reproduced by permission of the publisher, Candlewick Press, Somerville, MA.

32. **The Hippopotamus,** Hilaire Belloc.

34. **The Horses,** Maxine Kumin © 1972.

34. **The Horseman,** Walter de la Mare.

35. **Horses,** Aileen Fisher. From *Always Wondering: Some Favorite Poems of Aileen Fisher.* Copyright © 1991 Aileen Fisher. Reprinted by permission of Marian Reiner on behalf of the Boulder Public Library Foundation, Inc.

35. **The White Horse,** D. H. Lawrence.

37. **Mountain Gorilla,** Janet S. Wong. From *Once Upon A Tiger: New Beginnings for Endangered Animals* by Janet S. Wong. Copyright © 2011 by Janet S. Wong. Reproduced by permission of the author.

THE LITTLE ONES

40. **Ladybug,** Rebecca Kai Dotlich. From *Lemonade Sun and Other Summer Poems* by Rebecca Kai Dotlich. Copyright © 1998 by Rebecca Kai Dotlich. Published by Wordsong, an imprint of Boyds Mills Press. Reprinted by permission.

41. **Ants,** Marilyn Singer. Reprinted with the permission of Atheneum Books for Young Readers, an imprint of Simon and Schuster Children's Publishing Division from *Fireflies At Midnight* by Marilyn Singer. Text copyright © 2003 Marilyn Singer.

41. **Solitude,** Charles Simic. From *Selected Early Poems* by Charles Simic. Copyright © 1999 by Charles Simic. Reprinted by permission of George Braziller, Inc., New York.

42. **Dragonfly,** Georgia Heard. From *Creatures of Earth, Sea and Sky* by Georgia Heard. Copyright © 1992 by Georgia Heard. Published by Wordsong, an imprint of Boyds Mills Press. Reprinted by permission.

43. **Grasshoppers Three,** an old song.

45. **Little Fish,** D. H. Lawrence.

46. **The Caterpillar,** Douglas Florian. From *Insectlopedia: Poems and Paintings* by Douglas Florian. Copyright © 1998 by Douglas Florian. Reprinted by permission of Harcourt Children's Books, an imprint of Houghton Mifflin Harcourt Publishing Company. All rights reserved.

46. **Caterpillar,** Tony Johnston. From *In Small Talk: A Book of Short Poems.* © 1995. Reproduced by permission of Writers House.

47. **The Butterfly,** John Fuller. By permission of John Fuller and United Agents.

47. **Butterfly,** Benjamin Franklin.

48. **Cockroach sandwich,** Colin McNaughton, *Making Friends With Frankenstein.* Copyright © 1999 by Colin McNaughton. Reproduced by permission of the publisher, Candlewick Press, Somerville, MA.

48. **The Scorpion,** Hilaire Belloc.

49. **Inchworm,** Michael J. Rosen. By permission of the author, Michael J. Rosen, 2012.

49. **Inch by Inch,** Rebecca Kai Dotlich. Copyright © 2012 by Rebecca Kai Dotlich. Reprinted by permission of Curtis Brown, Ltd.

49. **Rich Lizard,** Deborah Chandra. *From Rich Lizard and Other Poems* by Deborah Chandra, illustrations by Leslie Bowman. Text copyright © 1993 by Deborah Chandra. Reprinted by permission of Farrar, Straus and Giroux, LLC.

50. **The Chipmunk,** Ogden Nash. Copyright © 1952 by Ogden Nash, renewed. First appeared in *Saturday Evening Post*. Reprinted by permission of Curtis Brown, Ltd.

51. **Spruce Woods,** A. R. Ammons. From *Worldly Hopes* by A. R. Ammons. Copyright © 1982 by A. R. Ammons. Used by permission of W. W. Norton and Company, Inc.

51. **Squirrel Forgets,** Lilian Moore. From *Adam Mouse's Book of Poems* by Lilian Moore. Copyright © 1992 Lilian Moore. Used by permission of Marian Reiner.

52. **Polliwogs,** Kristine O'Connell George. From *The Great Frog Race and Other Poems* by Kristine O'Connell George. Text copyright © 1997 by Kristine O'Connell George. Reprinted by permission of Clarion Books, an imprint of Houghton Mifflin Harcourt Publishing Company. All rights reserved.

53. **Oh the Toe-Test!,** Norma Farber. Copyright © 1969 and 1971 by Norma Farber. Used by permission of HarperCollins Publishers.

55. **The Spider Is a Lovely Lady,** Frank Asch. From *Sawgrass Poems: A View of the Everglades* by Frank Asch. Copyright © 1996 by Frank Asch. Reprinted by permission of Harcourt Children's Books, an imprint of Houghton Mifflin Harcourt Publishing Company. All rights reserved.

56. **I Am a Snail,** Anonymous.

56. **From The Snail,** William Cowper.

56. Riddle, Mary Ann Hoberman. From *The Llama Who Had No Pajama: 100 Favorite Poems* by Mary Ann Hoberman. Copyright © 1973 by Mary Ann Hoberman. Reprinted by permission of Harcourt Children's Books, an imprint of Houghton Mifflin Harcourt Publishing Company. All rights reserved.

56. Snail, X. J. Kennedy. Copyright © 1972 by X. J. Kennedy. First appeared in *Exploding Gravy*, published by Little, Brown. Reprinted by permission of Curtis Brown, Ltd.

57. Bee, X. J. Kennedy, Copyright © 1982 by X. J. Kennedy. First appeared in *Did Adam Name the Vinegarroon?*, published by David R. Godine Publishers. Reprinted by permission of Curtis Brown, Ltd.

57. Move Over, Lilian Moore. From *Little Raccoon and Poems from the Woods* by Lilian Moore. Copyright © 1975 Lilian Moore. Used by permission of Marian Reiner.

57. The Pedigree of Honey, Emily Dickinson.

57. A Bee, Matsuo Basho (Translation by Robert Hass). From *The Essential Haiku: Versions of Basho, Buson, and Issa*. Ecco Press. Reprinted by permission of the author.

58. A Mouse of My Acquaintance, Anonymous.

58. The City Mouse and the Garden Mouse, Christina Georgina Rossetti.

59. Hamster Hide-and-Seek, Avis Harley. From *A Pet for Me*. Copyright © 2003 by Avis Harley. Reprinted by permission of the author.

THE WINGED ONES

62. Three Little Owls Who Sang Hymns, Anonymous.

63. A Wise Old Owl, a nursery rhyme, Anonymous.

63. Haiku (Owl/syllable of wind), Anonymous.

63. I Talk with the Moon, Beverly McLoughland. Originally appeared in *Instructor*, May, 1985. Author controls all rights.

64. Gray Goose, Julie Larrios. From *Yellow Elephant: A Bright Bestiary With Poems* by Julie Larrios. Copyright © 2006 by Julie Larrios. Reprinted by permission of Harcourt Children's Books, an imprint of Houghton Mifflin Harcourt Publishing Company. All rights reserved.

64. Moon Geese, Ann Turner. Copyright © 1994 by Ann Turner. First appeared in *A Moon for Seasons*, published by Macmillan. Reprinted by permission of Curtis Brown, Ltd.

65. What Was That? David L. Harrison. From *Goose Lake*, an e-book by David L. Harrison.

65. De Grey Goose. Words and music by Huddie Ledbetter. Collected and adapted by John A. Lomax and Alan Lomax. TRO-© Copyright 1936 (renewed) Folkways Music Publishers, Inc. and Global Jukebox Publishing (BMI). TRO Folkways Music Publishers, Inc. controls all rights for the world outside the U.S.A. International copyright secured. Used by permission.

65. Puzzling, William Cole. Copyright © 1978 by William Cole. First appeared in *An Arkful of Animals*. Reprinted by permission of Curtis Brown, Ltd.

66. Blue Jay, Janet S. Wong. Copyright © 2012 by Janet S. Wong. Reproduced by permission of the author.

67. The Blackbird, Humbert Wolfe.

67. Dust of Snow, Robert Frost. From the book *The Poetry of Robert Frost*, edited by Edward Connery Lathem. Copyright © 1923, 1969 by Henry Holt and Company, copyright © 1951 by Robert Frost. Reprinted by permission of Henry Holt and Company, LLC.

69. The Eagle, Alfred, Lord Tennyson.

70. Mother's Plea, Lee Bennett Hopkins. Copyright © 1995 by Lee Bennett Hopkins. First appeared in *Good Rhymes, Good Times*, published by HarperCollins. Reprinted by permission of Curtis Brown, Ltd.

71. Coastal Bats, Calef Brown. © Calef Brown, 2012.

72. A Warbler, Walter de la Mare. Reproduced by permission of The Literary Trustees of Walter de la Mare and The Society of Authors.

72. The Saddest Noise, Emily Dickinson.

72. Birds in the Garden, Anonymous.

72. From Sing-Song, Christina Georgina Rossetti.

75. Inuit Song, translated by Edward Field, after Nakasuk. By permission of Edward Field.

75. Haiku (Sandpiper), Anonymous.

76. You Can Talk About Your Hummingbirds, Arnold Adoff. © 2012 by Arnold Adoff. Used by permission.

76. Visitor, Kristine O'Connell George. *Hummingbird Nest: A Journal of Poems* by Kristine O'Connell George. Copyright © 2004 by Kristine O'Connell George. Reprinted by permission of Harcourt Children's Books, an imprint of Houghton Mifflin Harcourt Publishing Company. All rights reserved.

76. Hummingbird, Janet S. Wong. Copyright © 2012 by Janet S. Wong. Reproduced by permission of the author.

78. Haiku (Sparrows), J. W. Hackett. World-famous, prize-winning haiku by permission of the author, J. W. Hackett, 2012.

79. Arrivals, Ann Turner. Copyright © 1994 by Ann Turner. First appeared in *A Moon for Seasons*, published by Macmillan. Reprinted by permission of Curtis Brown, Ltd.

80. The White Egret, Paul Janeczko. By permission of the author, Paul Janeczko.

81. The Parrot, Anonymous.

THE WATER ONES

84. The Penguin, Oliver Herford.

84. Penguins, Charles Ghigna. By permission of the author, Charles Ghigna, for "Penguins" from *Animal Tracks: Wild Poems To Read Aloud*. Copyright © 2004 by Charles Ghigna. Published by Harry N. Abrams.

85. Lost in the Cold, Anonymous.

86. Anemone, Jane Yolen. Copyright © 1996 by Jane Yolen. First appeared in *Sea Watch*, published by Philomel Books. Reprinted by permission of Curtis Brown, Ltd.

87. The Starfish, David McCord. From *Far and Few* by David McCord. Copyright © 1952 by David McCord. By permission of Little, Brown and Company and the estate of David J. W. McCord. All rights reserved.

88. Seal, William Jay Smith. From *Laughing Time: Collected Nonsense* by William Jay Smith. Copyright © 1990 by William Jay Smith. Reprinted by permission of Farrar, Straus and Giroux, LLC.

89. The Performing Seal, Rachel Field.

89. Seal Lullaby, Rudyard Kipling.

90. The Walrus, Jack Prelutsky. Copyright © 1983 by Jack Prelutsky. Used by permission of HarperCollins Publishers.

90. The Eel, Ogden Nash. Copyright © 1941 by Ogden Nash, renewed. First appeared in *New Yorker*. Reprinted by permission of Curtis Brown, Ltd.

91. Beavers in November, Marilyn Singer. © Marilyn Singer. From *Turtles in July*, Macmillan, 1989.

92. There Was an Old Person of Hyde, Edward Lear.

93. Young Prince Pinch, Avis Harley. From *The Monarch's Progress* by Avis Harley. Copyright © 2008 by Avis Harley. Published by Wordsong, an imprint of Boyds Mills Press. Reprinted by permission.

93. The Crab, Conrad Aiken. From *Cats and Bats and Things With Wings* by Conrad Aiken. Atheneum Publishers. Copyright © 1965 by Conrad Aiken. Copyright renewed © 1993 by Joan Aiken and Jane Aiken Hodge. Used by permission of Brandt and Hochman Literary Agents, Inc.

94. Happy the Ocean, Anonymous.

95. Sea Turtle, Anonymous.

95. Turtles, Charles Ghigna. By permission of the author. From *Animal Tracks: Wild Poems to Read Aloud*. Copyright © 2004 by Charles Ghigna. Published by Harry N. Abrams.

96. The Shark, Lord Alfred Douglas, © John Rubinstein and John Stratford, Literary Executors of Lord Alfred Douglas; all rights reserved.

97. About the Teeth of Sharks, John Ciardi. Copyright © 1962 by John Ciardi. Used by permission of HarperCollins Publishers.

98. Sea Jelly, Kelly Ramsdell Fineman. By permission of the author, Kelly Ramsdell Fineman, 2012.

99. Do Oysters Sneeze?, Jack Prelutsky. Copyright © 1984 by Jack Prelutsky. Used by permission of HarperCollins Publishers.

99. Mussel, Steven Withrow.

100. Don't Call Alligator Long-Mouth Till You Cross River, John Agard.

Copyright © 1986 by John Agard reproduced by kind permission of John Agard c/o Caroline Sheldon Literary Agency Limited.

101. **The Crocodile,** Lewis Carroll.

101. **Dark Meat,** Anonymous.

THE STRANGE ONES

104. **Moray Eel,** Steven Withrow.

105. **All You Oughta Know About a Piranha,** Michael J. Rosen. By permission of the author, Michael J. Rosen, 2012.

106. **The Ostrich,** Ogden Nash. Copyright © 1956 by Ogden Nash, renewed. First appeared in *New Yorker.* Reprinted by permission of Curtis Brown, Ltd.

106. **The Ostrich Is a Silly Bird,** Mary E. Wilkins Freeman.

107. **I Am a Baby Porcupette,** Joyce Sidman. From *Dark Emperor and Other Poems* by Joyce Sidman. Copyright © 2010 by Joyce Sidman. Reprinted by permission of Houghton Mifflin Harcourt Publishing Company. All rights reserved.

107. **Porcupine,** Rebecca Kai Dotlich. Copyright © 2002 by Rebecca Kai Dotlich. Reprinted by permission of Curtis Brown, Ltd.

108. **The Octopus,** Ogden Nash, "The Octopus" Copyright © 1941 by Ogden Nash, renewed. First appeared in *New Yorker.* Reprinted by permission of Curtis Brown, Ltd.

109. **Seahorse,** Blake Morrison. Reproduced from @ Blake Morrison 1991 by permission of United Agents Ltd. (www.unitedagents.co.uk) on behalf of Blake Morrison.

110. **What Is the Opposite of Pillow?,** Richard Wilbur. From *More Opposites: Poems and Drawings* by Richard Wilbur. Copyright © 1991 by Richard Wilbur. Reprinted by permission of Harcourt Children's Books, an imprint of Houghton Mifflin Harcourt Publishing Company. All rights reserved.

111. **The Argument,** Bobbi Katz. Copyright © 2012 by Bobbi Katz.

111. **The Anteater,** Douglas Florian. From *Insectlopedia: Poems and Paintings* by Douglas Florian. Copyright © 1994 by Douglas Florian. Reprinted by permission of Harcourt Children's Books, an imprint of Houghton Mifflin Harcourt Publishing Company. All rights reserved.

112. **Travel Plans,** Bobbi Katz, Copyright © 2012 by Bobbi Katz.

113. **The Meerkats of Africa,** Gavin Ewart. By permission of the Gavin Ewart Estate.

114. **Sand Ghost,** Betsy Franco. By permission of the author, Betsy Franco, 2012.

115. **Frilled Lizard,** Alice Schertl. Used by permission of the author, who controls all rights.

116. **The Yak,** Hilaire Belloc.

116. **How to Tell a Camel,** J. Patrick Lewis. First published in *A Hippopotamusn't,* Dial, 1990. Copyright © J. Patrick Lewis, 1990.

117. **Skunk,** Lilian Moore, "Skunk Won't Shrink" was originally titled "Skunk" and is from *Adam Mouse's Book of Poems* by Lilian Moore. Copyright © 1992 Lilian Moore. Used by permission of Marian Reiner.

118. **A Flamingo Is,** J. Patrick Lewis. First published in *A Hippopotamusn't,* Dial, 1990. Copyright © J. Patrick Lewis, 1990.

119. **A Blue-Footed Booby,** Michael J. Rosen. By permission of the author, Michael J. Rosen, 2012.

119. **Spoonbill Haiku,** Jane Yolen. From *A Mirror to Nature: Poems About Reflection,* written by Jane Yolen. Copyright © 2009 by Jane Yolen and Jason Stemple. Published by Wordsong, an imprint of Boyds Mills Press. Reprinted by permission of Boyds Mills Press and Curtis Brown Ltd.

120. **How to Paint a Zebra,** Anonymous.

120. **Zebra,** Gavin Ewart. By permission of the Gavin Ewart Estate.

121. **Zebra,** Judith Thurman. From *Flashlight and Other Poems* by Judith Thurman. Copyright © 1976 by Judith Thurman. Used by permission of Marian Reiner.

121. **A Promise,** Bobbi Katz. Copyright © 2012 by Bobbi Katz.

122. **A Centipede Was Happy Quite,** Anonymous.

122. **Vanishing Act,** Tracie Vaughn Zimmer. By permission of the author, Tracie Vaughn Zimmer, 2012.

123. **Proboscis Monkey Ponders Man,** Alice Schertle. Used by permission of the author, Alice Schertle, who controls all rights.

THE NOISY ONES

127. **The Frog,** Hilaire Belloc.

129. **The Bull,** Alice Schertle. From *How Now, Brown Cow?* by Alice Schertle. Copyright © 1994 by Alice Schertle. Reprinted by permission of Harcourt Children's Books, an imprint of Houghton Mifflin Harcourt Publishing Company. All rights reserved.

129. **Bull and Ox,** Anonymous.

130. **Crickets,** Myra Cohn Livingston. From *I Never Told and Other Poems* by Myra Cohn Livingston. Copyright © 1992 by Myra Cohn Livingston. All rights reserved. Reprinted by permission of Marian Reiner.

131. **Splinter,** Carl Sandburg. From *Harvest Poems 1910–1960* by Carl Sandburg. Copyright © 1928, and renewed 1956 by Carl Sandburg. Reprinted by permission of Houghton Mifflin Harcourt Publishing Company. All rights reserved.

131. **Crickets,** Harry Behn. From *Crickets and Bullfrogs and Whispers of Thunder* by Harry Behn. Copyright 1949, 1953, 1956, 1957, 1966, 1968 by Harry Behn. Copyright renewed 1977 by Alice L. Behn. Copyright renewed 1981 by Alice Behn Goebel, Pamela Behn Adam, Prescott Behn, and Peter Behn. Used by permission of Marian Reiner.

132. **Why Pigs Cannot Write Poems,** John Ciardi. From *Doodle Soup: Poems by John Ciardi.* Copyright © 1985 by Myra J. Ciardi. Reprinted by permission of Houghton Mifflin Harcourt Publishing Company. All rights reserved.

132. **Pig,** Richard Edwards. *Moon Frog: Animal Poems for Young Children.* Copyright © 1992 Richard Edwards. Reproduced by permission of the publisher, Candlewick Press, Somerville, MA.

133. **Piety,** Ambrose Bierce.

133. **Summertime,** Myra Cohn Livingston. Copyright © 1995 by Myra Cohn Livingston. All rights reserved. Reprinted by permission of Marian Reiner.

134. **Unpopular Rex,** X. J. Kennedy. Copyright © 1985 by X. J. Kennedy. First appeared in *The Forgetful Wishing Well: Poems for Young People,* published by Atheneum. Reprinted by permission of Curtis Brown, Ltd.

134. **Dog,** Naomi Shihab Nye. By permission of the author, Naomi Shihab Nye, 2012.

135. **The Breed You Need,** Bobbi Katz. Copyright © 2012 by Bobbi Katz.

136. **The Greater Cats,** V. Sackville-West. Reproduced with permission of Curtis Brown Group Ltd, London on behalf of The Estate of Vita Sackville-West, 1929.

136. **You've Got Male,** Avis Harley. From *Fly with Poetry: An ABC of Poetry* by Avis Harley. Copyright © 2006 by Avis Harley. Published by Wordsong, an imprint of Boyds Mills Press. Reprinted by permission.

136. **Lion,** Janet S. Wong. Reprinted with the permission of Margaret K. McElderry Books, an imprint of Simon and Schuster Children's Publishing Division, from *Twist: Yoga Poems* by Janet S. Wong. Text copyright © 2007 Janet S. Wong.

138. **A Picture of the Rooster,** Tang Yin.

139. **Raccoon,** Janet S. Wong. Copyright © 2012 by Janet S. Wong. Reproduced by permission of the author.

140. **From Road-Song of the Bandar-Log,** Rudyard Kipling.

142. **From The Law of the Jungle,** Rudyard Kipling

143. **Why Wolves Howl,** Anonymous.

145. **Jack A.,** J. Patrick Lewis. First published in *A Hippopotamusn't,* Dial, 1990. Copyright © J. Patrick Lewis, 1990.

145. **The Donkey,** a nursery rhyme.

145. **Visiting an Old Friend,** Charles Waters. Copyright © 2012 by the author, who controls all rights.

THE QUIET ONES

148. **Rabbit,** Mary Ann Hoberman. From *The Llama Who Had No Pajama: 100 Favorite Poems* by Mary Ann Hoberman. Copyright © 1973 by Mary Ann

photo credits

Hoberman. Reprinted by permission of Harcourt Children's Books, an imprint of Houghton Mifflin Harcourt Publishing Company. All rights reserved.

149. **Four Ducks on a Pond**, William Allingham.

150. **Firefly**, Elizabeth Madox Roberts.

151. **Luna Moth**, J. Patrick Lewis. First published in *Ridicholas Nicholas: More Animal Poems*, Dial 1995. Copyright © J. Patrick Lewis, 1990.

151. **The Warning**, Adelaide Crapsey.

152. **Home to Roost**, Kay Ryan. By permission of the author, Kay Ryan, 2012.

153. **The Hens**, Elizabeth Madox Roberts.

153. **Haiku (chicken)**, Kristine O'Connell George, who controls all rights.

154. **Cat in the Snow**, Aileen Fisher. From *My Cat Has Eyes of Sapphire Blue* by Aileen Fisher. Copyright © 1973 Aileen Fisher. Reprinted by permission of Marian Reiner on behalf of the Boulder Public Library Foundation, Inc.

154. **Fog**, Carl Sandburg.

154. **Haiku (cat)**, Avis Harley. From *Sea Stars: Saltwater Poems* by Avis Harley. Copyright © 2006 by Avis Harley. Published by Wordsong, an imprint of Boyds Mills Press. Reprinted by permission.

154. **Two Cats**, Anonymous.

155. **Sunning**, James S. Tippett. Copyright © 1933 by Harper and Row. Renewed 1961 by Martha Tippett. Used by permission of HarperCollins Publishers.

156. **Pet Snake**, Rebecca Kai Dotlich. Copyright © 2003 by Rebecca Kai Dotlich. Reprinted by permission of Curtis Brown, Ltd.

156. **Dressing Like a Snake**, Georgia Heard. From *Creatures of Earth, Sea and Sky* by Georgia Heard. Copyright © 1992 by Georgia Heard. Published by Wordsong, an imprint of Boyds Mills Press. Reprinted by permission.

156. **Snake**, Barbara Juster Esbensen. From *Words With Wrinkled Knees: Animal Poems* by Barbara Juster Esbensen. Copyright © 1998 by Barbara Juster Esbensen. Published by Wordsong, an imprint of Boyds Mills Press. Reprinted by permission.

158. **The Panther**, Ogden Nash. Copyright © 1940 by Ogden Nash, renewed. First appeared in *Saturday Evening Post*. Reprinted by permission of Curtis Brown, Ltd.

159. **Coyote Landscape**, Jane Yolen. From *A Mirror to Nature: Poems About Reflection*, written by Jane Yolen. Copyright © 2009 by Jane Yolen and Jason Stemple. Published by Wordsong, an imprint of Boyds Mills Press. Reprinted by permission of Boyds Mills Press and Curtis Brown Ltd.

160. **I Saw a Sloth Play Soccer**, Kenn Nesbitt. Copyright 2012, Kenn Nesbitt. All rights reserved. From *The Tighty-Whitey Spider: And More Wacky Animal Poems I Totally Made Up*. Sourcebooks Jabberwocky. Reprinted by permission of the author.

161. **From I Have Lived and I Have Loved** (Excerpt), Charles Mackay.

162. **'I Am Home,' Said the Turtle**, John Ciardi. From *Doodle Soup: Poems by John Ciardi*. Copyright © 1985 by Myra J. Ciardi. Reprinted by permission of Houghton Mifflin Harcourt Publishing Company. All rights reserved.

163. **Box Turtle**, Joyce Sidman. By permission of the author, Joyce Sidman.

163. **The Tortoise**, Joan Bransfield Graham. Copyright © 2012 Joan Bransfield Graham. Used by permission of the author, who controls all rights.

FINAL THOUGHT

164. **Animals**, Walt Whitman.

166. **Hurt No Living Thing**, Christina Georgina Rossetti.

167. **Magic Words**, Inuit poem, translated by Edward Field. By permission of Edward Field.

169. **Make the Earth Your Companion**, J. Patrick Lewis. First published in *Earth and Me: Our Family Tree*, Dawn Publications, 2002. Copyright © J. Patrick Lewis, 2002.

170 and 171 and trade case cover. All poems by J. Patrick Lewis. Published by permission of the author.

Back cover, **Travel Plans**, Bobbi Katz, Copyright © 2012 by Bobbi Katz.

Published by the National Geographic Society
John M. Fahey, Jr., Chairman of the Board and
    Chief Executive Officer
Timothy T. Kelly, President
Declan Moore, Executive Vice President; President,
    Publishing and Digital Media
Melina Gerosa Bellows, Executive Vice President; Chief Cre-
    ative Officer, Books, Kids, and Family

Prepared by the Book Division
Hector Sierra, Senior Vice President
    and General Manager
Nancy Laties Feresten, Senior Vice President,
    Editor in Chief, Children's Books
Jonathan Halling, Design Director, Books
    and Children's Publishing
Jay Sumner, Director of Photography,
    Children's Publishing
Jennifer Emmett, Editorial Director,
    Children's Books
Eva Absher-Schantz, Managing Art Director
Carl Mehler, Director of Maps
R. Gary Colbert, Production Director
Jennifer A. Thornton, Director of Managing Editorial

Staff for This Book
Jennifer Emmett, Project Editor
Lori Epstein, Senior Illustrations Editor
Eva Absher-Schantz, Designer
Grace Hill, Associate Managing Editor
Joan Gossett, Production Editor
Lewis R. Bassford, Production Manager
Susan Borke, Legal and Business Affairs
Holly Marshall and Caroline Couig, Rights Clearance
Kate Olesin, Assistant Editor
Kathryn Robbins, Design Production Assistant
Hillary Moloney, Illustrations Assistant

Manufacturing and Quality Management
Christopher A. Liedel, Chief Financial Officer
Phillip L. Schlosser, Senior Vice President
Chris Brown, Vice President
George Bounelis, Vice President, Production Services
Nicole Elliott, Manager
Rachel Faulise, Manager
Robert L. Barr, Manager

The National Geographic Society is one of the
world's largest nonprofit scientific and educational
organizations. Founded in 1888 to "increase and
diffuse geographic knowledge," the Society works
to inspire people to care about the planet. National
Geographic reflects the world through its magazines,
television programs, films, music and radio, books, DVDs, maps,
exhibitions, live events, school publishing programs, interac-
tive media and merchandise. *National Geographic* magazine,
the Society's official journal, published in English and 33
local-language editions, is read by more than 38 million people
each month. The National Geographic Channel reaches 320
million households in 34 languages in 166 countries. National
Geographic Digital Media receives more than 15 million visitors
a month. National Geographic has funded more than 9,400
scientific research, conservation and exploration projects and
supports an education program promoting geography literacy.
For more information, visit nationalgeographic.com.

For more information, please call
1-800-NGS LINE (647-5463) or
write to the following address:
National Geographic Society
1145 17th Street N.W.
Washington, D.C. 20036-4688 U.S.A.

Visit us online at www.nationalgeographic.com/books

For librarians and teachers:
www.ngchildrensbooks.org

More for kids from National Geographic:
kids.nationalgeographic.com

For information about special discounts for bulk purchases, please
contact National Geographic Books Special Sales:
ngspecsales@ngs.org

For rights or permissions inquiries, please contact National
Geographic Books Subsidiary Rights:
ngbookrights@ngs.org

Library of Congress Cataloging-in-Publication Data

National Geographic book of animal poetry : 200 poems with pho-
tographs that squeak, soar, and roar / [edited by] J. Patrick Lewis.
      p. cm.
Includes bibliographical references and index.
ISBN 978-1-4263-1009-6 (hardcover : alk. paper)
ISBN 978-1-4263-1054-6 (library binding : alk. paper)
1. Animals--Poetry. I. Lewis, J. Patrick.
PN6110.A7N46 2012
808.81'936--dc23
                                                2012010404

Acknowledgments
To the entire National Geographic team for their enthusiasm
and dedication in the making of this book, and to all the poets
whose deserving work, regrettably, could not be squeezed into its
pages.—JPL

The publisher gratefully acknowledges the heroic efforts of
Caroline Couig and Holly Marshall in securing permissions, as
well as the invaluable assistance of editorial interns Susie Charlop,
Molly Gasparre, Libby Marsh, Eileen McFarland, and Maura Welch.

Printed in China
12/TS/1

To poets, animals, and animal poets everywhere—JPL

LABRADOR RETRIEVER